Called Into Now

Cycle A Sermons Based on Second Lessons
for Advent, Christmas, and Epiphany

Heather Sugden

CSS Publishing Company, Inc.
Lima, Ohio

CALLED INTO NOW

FIRST EDITION
Copyright © 2022
by CSS Publishing Co., Inc.

Library of Congress Cataloging-in-Publication Data:

Names: Sugden, Heather, author.
Title: Called into now : cycle A sermons based on the second lessons for
   Advent, Christmas, and Epiphany / Heather Sugden.
Description: Lima, Ohio : CSS Publishing Company, Inc., 2022.
Identifiers: LCCN 2022010783 (print) ǀ LCCN 2022010784 (ebook) ǀ ISBN
   9780788030567 (paperback) ǀ ISBN 9780788030574 (adobe pdf)
Subjects: LCSH: Bible. New Testament--Sermons. ǀ Advent sermons. ǀ
   Christmas sermons. ǀ Epiphany--Sermons. ǀ Common lectionary (1992). Year A.
Classification: LCC BS2341.55 .S84 2022 (print) ǀ LCC BS2341.55 (ebook) ǀ
   DDC 252/.612--dc23/eng/20220608
LC record available at https://lccn.loc.gov/2022010783
LC ebook record available at https://lccn.loc.gov/2022010784

For more information about CSS Publishing Company resources, visit our website at www.csspub.com, email us at csr@csspub.com, or call (800) 241-4056.

e-book:
ISBN-13: 978-0-7880-3057-4
ISBN-10: 0-7880-3057-4

ISBN-13: 978-0-7880-3056-7
ISBN-10: 0-7880-3056-6

Contents

Introduction

As I have been working on this series of sermons, the words of urgency have sprung from the pages of the New Testament and found a place in our world today. We who have lived through a pandemic, who have seen our churches and our daily routines turned upside down, are now desperately seeking some sense of return to normal and hope for the future. And yet, we also understand that the world is not the same as it was before, and that we are not the same people we were before isolation and the peculiar devastation of Covid-19 brought into our world.

Such a confluence that past, present, and future shapes the writings from the early church. These early Christian words stand as both encouragement and a call to action, as the church is challenged to lean into the urgency of their day while also not being afraid.

We, too, would do well to follow the advice of these writings. We are to avoid quarreling, stop placing labels on one another that lend themselves to a hierarchy, and try at all times to follow the example of Jesus as servant.

I wish I had a clearer vision of exactly where the church is headed. But I do trust and believe that these ancient words can guide us as we move together in following Jesus.

In Christ,
Heather Sugden

Do We REALLY Know What Time It Is?

Years ago, I was staying in a hotel near the airport in anticipation of an early morning flight the next day. The hotel had an alarm clock in the room, and, being an independent type, I decided to set the alarm myself rather than bother the staff member at the front desk for a wake-up call.

This was before the days of wide spread cell phones, when nightstands in hotels often had clock radios with built-in alarms. This episode happened so long ago, in fact, that a person needed to talk with another human person in order to check in and out of the hotel!

Setting my own alarm clock really was an effort to be independent and not bother the hotel staff. But if I were to be completely honest, my thinking was not only sparing work for the hotel clerk. I believe part of my motivation was control, too. By running the alarm clock myself, I would not have to depend on this person at the front desk. I would not have to worry about the staff member forgetting to call me, or giving up if I did not wake up right away. Who knew if this person was reliable or not? Who knew if they would even care if I stressed out about rushing all around and being late? Surely I was capable of waking myself up better than a stranger who had no interest in whether or not I got up in time to catch my flight!

To prepare for the early wake up, I went to bed early, making sure to close the heavy hotel curtains tightly against the lights in the parking lot. I packed up whatever belongings I would not need in the morning before turning out the final lamp in my room. I checked the alarm clock one last time before closing my eyes. I managed to fall asleep by telling myself that I had done everything I could to make the coming morning seamless and productive.

It was the dark of night when the blare of the alarm clock went off like a freight train through my dreams. My arm instinctively swatted the machine until it stopped screaming. I got up out of bed and went through my morning routine as if a computer was running its morning program update: showering, dressing, and packing up my belongings in rapid succession, until checking the room one last time before stepping out into the hotel hallway.

Since I knew my wake-up time was early, my body was still half asleep, my eyes only half-focused. It did not seem strange that all was dark as I left my room. It did not strike me as odd that the hallways were silent. The hotel had many of the same sights, sounds, and artificial lighting as it had at any time of the day or night.

Only when I got to the front desk and saw the clock above the desk did I realize that it was one o'clock in the morning, and not six a.m., as I had expected.

I stood at the desk in shock, simply staring at the time as its reality slowly sank into my nighttime brain. I trudged back to my room, suitcase dragging behind me even more slowly than before — a picture of defeat rather than the triumph of purposeful planning. I lay back in bed, fully dressed. There was no point in pretending to have a normal routine now!

How could I make such a mistake? How could I mess up the time so badly?

Obviously, I had made an error somewhere in my planning process. Did I set the alarm clock incorrectly? Was the clock's time off? Why did I not check my watch at any point during my "morning" routine? How could I so easily fall into line with such a false sense of what time it truly was?

I guess it is all too easy to be fooled in the confusion of waking up. I imagine it is all too easy for any of us to lose our bearings when it comes to time. The fog of early morning, the bleary eyes of a long night, the dullness of waiting for the expected first rays of dawn can all play with our internal clock and alter our sense of urgency.

When Paul wrote to the early Christian community in Rome, his words on time invited them into a shared urgency. "You know what time it is," Paul wrote. According to Paul, it was time to wake up and to live a life that showed forth their faith. The time, he assured anyone who was listening, was *then*. A broader reading of Paul's life and the life of the early church fleshes out the reality of their sense of time. Any day they could face death because of their Christian faith. Any hour could bring accusation and trial. Any moment could be their last on Earth.

While the threat of impending death might paralyze us, Paul's reaction was to move full-speed ahead. Believers were to not hide in the dark — putting their Christian identity aside, denying their faith, or seeking to blend in with the world-at-large. No, Paul urged, they were to boldly accept the calling of the moment in which they found themselves, and come out into the bright light of day.

Paul's ethic showed forth in this passage, too. Those living in the faith will reject "reveling and drunkenness.... debauchery and licentiousness... quarreling and jealousy" and instead live boldly a life worthy of followers of Christ.

Imagine "putting on the armor of light" as a metaphor for baptism. Just as the baptized physically clothe themselves in white gowns even in modern times, a newly baptized Christian should be identifiable even when moving about outside of the baptismal gathering. Their actions, their efforts, their desire to do what is honorable in the eyes of God mark them as distinct from the rest of the world.

In their actions and in the boldness of their actions, Christians should also make full use of the time they have in this world. Their everyday choices in how to live will separate this time from any other.

So what are we to make of the urgency in Paul's writings as we sit here today? While we hear many loud shouts even now declaring end times, we have largely learned to leave such warnings to the realm of metaphors. We know that Jesus did not return in Paul's lifetime. We still confess that we are waiting for Jesus to come again. Is it possible to wait with urgency for 2,000 years?

Advent is a time of urgent waiting. For most of us, this is an alarm we have set for ourselves. We feel the urgency of a cultural push that will pick up speed as we get closer to Christmas.

Can you feel the push to buy? Do you hear the clock ticking on the "days until Christmas"? Are you counting time by the number of activities you have to complete, events you must attend, gifts you need to wrap, cards that demand to be written, addressed, and dropped in the mail so that they arrive before Christmas?

The weeks before Christmas can both frighten and excite us with a countdown we have established as a society to emphasize consumerism and busy-ness. Even with the best of intentions, we can contort the days ahead of us into a limited opportunity to densely pack in as many memories and as much meaning as possible. The result, of course, is stress of such magnitude that we simply feel tired, grumpy, detached from real meaning. We might even just "want to get it over with."

How often our desire is to control time — to bend it to our will — to declare what we want to do — that this is our moment(!) — rather than seeing time as a gift from God which by its very nature we cannot control.

Yes — that blaring alarm clock of Paul's words to the Romans is not ours to set or turn off. It is for us to hear, and to know that the time for us to act is now.

An alarm sounding in our ears while we are sound asleep can be terrifying. The gift of light and truth in the darkness of complacency can also lead to urgent renewal.

What always strikes me in reading Paul's letters to the early Christian church is that urgency did not cause them fear, but instead seemed to bring them clarity and purpose. I wonder how clarity and purpose might help us in the time in which we find ourselves, particularly as we enter the season of Advent. I wonder also at our ability to stop — and listen — to the prophetic words before us today, which do call us into a moment which will fade.

One of the privileges of being a pastor is hearing the stories of Advent re-read and re-lived each year. Instead of being boring or blasé, they actually seem to grow in intensity, even if I do not know how to respond to the call to action in the here and now.

How can a 2,000 year old story still speak to us? How can it still be relevant? How, in the world, can it still be urgent?

I suppose the answers to all of those questions lie in the truth the stories show forth that speak directly to the questions of the here and now. We are still desperate for a savior. We still hide in darkness. We still find ourselves putting off what we know we should do or say. We still bat at the blaring alarm clock until it is silent, and do not bother to look around us at the signs of true time, and the journey into which we are called.

But God's story does not stop. No, this Advent we are reminded once again that God's story is ongoing, alive, active, and calling us into its light.

We could spend lots of time and invest great amounts of energy in defining what Paul means by calling us to "live honorably as in the day" and defining the actions that do and do not fit into such a calling. In fact, as church we have spent lots of time and great amounts of energy in calling out the sins we have defined in the world around us.

I think rather than make lists of who is "in" and who is "out" in terms of behavior, Paul's words to the Roman church sound an alarm ringing for us to open our eyes and live fully — right now.

What would it mean for us instead to wake up and truly believe that salvation was near? How would we live each day if we were wearing an armor of light? Who else would be drawn to the light of Christ if we truly "put on the Lord Jesus Christ" and lived honorably by loving our neighbor as we love ourselves?

The twinkling lights of this season tell us that Christmas is getting close. Can we as Christians proclaim that the light of this season is really a proclamation that salvation is nearer?

My brothers and sisters in Christ, we do know what time it is. We know that salvation is near. Shine brightly — shine the light of our Lord Jesus Christ to call all the world to wake up!

Amen.

Will You Sing With Me?

My congregation has a wonderful institutional history of Christmas caroling. As the story has been passed on down to me, there was a time when every Christmas Eve worship service was packed with families, and every moment in between Christmas Eve worship services was an opportunity for community caroling. We might not be certain when exactly this time was in our history, but we know it happened, we know that it was fantastic, and we profess our desire to return to such a time.

In these Christmas days of old, gangs of singers, gathered by age, relationship, and time choices made by family constraints, would bundle up in their winter warmest and brave the elements of the season, driving or walking from house to house, bringing cheer, the joy of music, and a wandering party atmosphere to each home and person they encountered.

I was so taken with the power and beauty of these memories of Christmases past that I thought it would be fun and meaningful to re-create them. Trying to re-create them was my first mistake.

"Christmas Eve is a time for families," I was told when I brought up the idea of caroling.

"We have to travel to dinner at this home, dessert in another. Our schedule is booked."

"It is the only day we have all the grandkids together."

"There's just not enough free time in between services."

"There just are not enough people to get a group together."

I agreed. They were all good reasons not to go caroling on Christmas Eve.

"Perhaps the Youth Group would want to carol," someone suggested. "Maybe they could cheer up the residents of the nursing home down the street."

That did sound like a good idea. We set a date and arranged with the long-term care facility for a spirit-filled visit in the month of December. We advertised, cajoled, and rounded up parents and children. We did what any great youth program does, and ordered crazy amounts of pizza to feed everyone after worship one Advent Sunday before we went out singing.

When someone asked if there was a songbook for us to follow, I made my second mistake.

"We don't need songbooks! Everyone knows Christmas songs!" I shouted.

Pride is a sin that shows up in many and various forms, including after the consumption of large amounts of pizza at youth gatherings.

The care facility down the street was more than happy to welcome us to their community room on a sunny Sunday afternoon. The place was already decorated for the season; the employees festive in holiday gear. The residents were lined up in neat rows — some in wheelchairs, some in zippy scooters with lights and whistles, some seated on the comfy couches of the common room. They were in various stages of alertness, as we had arrived directly after lunch and smack dab in the middle of prime napping time.

But all the residents' faces changed when the children walked in to the room. As I would repeat to my children many times following this day, "Isn't it amazing to be able to make someone smile only with your presence?" Children have this superpower. The residents were beaming, simply to have the youth group gathered in the same room as them.

Now it was time to provide some promised entertainment. Unfortunately, I am not a singer. I am also not a song leader. But I believed that Christmas songs were an exception to the rule — that anyone and everyone has permission to act silly, sing out loud, and be totally off-key when belting out yuletide joy at the top of their lungs.

I do not recall the first Christmas song I began to sing, but I quickly realized that my enthusiasm was not being matched by the youth singing all around me. I also realized that as charming as the youth were, no matter what they did, no one present that day really wanted to hear me sing Christmas songs all by myself.

I turned to loudly whisper to the youth I was leading, "Do you know the words to this song?" They did not have to say "no;" the frozen expressions on their faces gave me the answer immediately. "*O Little Town of Bethlehem*? *Joy to the World*? Surely you know *Silent Night*?" I pleaded. Nothing… "Ok, *Jingle Bells*? *Rudolph*? *Frosty the Snowman*?" Maybe it was stage fright, or maybe my fear was contagious, but the joyful noise of my youth group had suddenly gone quiet.

Luckily, the activities director of the facility was also a keen observer. She had already gone to her office and retrieved Christmas song books for us to use.

With words in hand, the festive mood quickly returned. We could and did sing the songs as a group — not only as a group of youth and leaders, but soon with residents' voices as well. The residents were inspired to join in, as if the act of singing had been contagious and they wanted to have as much fun and match the energy and joy of their visitors.

But I believe the residents wanted to join in on the singing because they felt they were teaching the words, too. They already knew all the words to the old and familiar songs — without the help of songbooks. It did not seem to matter that the residents' hearing had declined, that their eyes not as keen as before, their voices more feeble and their strength left to memory. They still remembered. They remembered the words to familiar Christmas songs, and their singing grew stronger to see young people singing as well.

That's the power of singing. When there are strong voices leading the singing, the quieter voices find it easier to blend in. And as the voices merge and blend together, a stronger, fuller, wider sound emerges that would have never been possible without the contribution of each and every voice singing out in that moment.

And while song books are helpful, to read the lyrics out of a book is very different from hearing the sound emerge and grow all around you and lead you to lift up your own voice. When a familiar song fills the room, we all sing with our whole self, and we all feel that the words become our own.

I wonder sometimes what songs I have passed on to the next generation. Have I sung songs that glorified wealth and lifted up the powerful? Have I hummed along to the familiar and all-too-common songs our culture sings? Have I taught the words to songs that I find helpful and meaningful in my life so that their lessons are passed on to others who do not yet know the words? Have I been loud enough in leading a song that goes against the assumed hum of busy-ness and obsession with wealth that seems to fill every silence in our world?

Because if I do not sing loudly and teach the songs of faith to those who do not yet know them, then I will also fail to remember the words myself.

In his letter to the Romans, Paul points to the words of scripture as a source of hope. He prays that God calls the community of that ancient church into "harmony with one another." In Christ, they may together "with one voice glorify the God and Father of our Lord Jesus Christ."

It sounds like a song, doesn't it? Paul's words paint the church as a choir, drawing upon scripture as their lyrics, singing together with one voice through the unity Christ brings, and yet reflecting the rich harmonies of a diverse community. We can imagine the full sound that swells from this church, rooted in God's Word and singing out loud the hope they have found in their faith.

Paul also quotes some of these ancient words of scripture to encourage his listeners: words of the prophet Isaiah and words of praise and joy. These are songs echoing from ancient times, repeated by ancestors of faith, sung loudly in life by song leaders who not only remembered the words of hope, but lived them loudly with their whole being.

When sung out loud to the church in Rome, the followers of Christ who hear these words cannot help but sing also. Gentile and Jew, slave and free, the quiet voices and the loud ones — now all singing together so that the words might not be forgotten.

Of course, it is not just Paul who will echo words known to us from the Old Testament. Jesus often quoted the scriptures in his ministry on Earth, drawing upon ancient words of hope and calls to change from the earliest prophets who sang God's music to all who would listen. His mother, upon learning of her pregnancy from the angel Gabriel, sings the words of *The Magnificat*, an ancient song of God's promise that echoes in her own life at that moment. As a faithful singer, we can only imagine the lullabies Mary sang to her baby, and the songs taught in Jesus' childhood home and synagogue. Without a doubt, songs of faith shaped Jesus into a loud singer for the world. His songs shape us into people who are willing to sing out loud for all to hear.

When we tell the story of Jesus, when we share it with those around us through word and through deed, our lives become a living song of hope. When the song is shared, others cannot help but listen to the lyrics, and be drawn into learning, repeating, and believing the words of faith.

So what songs are we teaching our youth? What songs do we know the words and melody so well that we are not afraid to sing loudly? Which songs bring forth such a chorus of voices that we are bold enough to add harmony and let the music grow and swell? What lyrics do we remember so well that we no longer need to read them from a book, but have them written in our memories and dwelling in our hearts for all time?

I have found that in the most trying times of my life, it is song to which I turn. Sleepless nights full of worry have brought forth "Give Me Jesus;" I hear "Amazing Grace" and tears fall; I am filled with joy and want to shout "Go Tell it on the Mountain." Songs my parents and grandparents sang to me come to my lips, even when I cannot exactly remember when or where I heard them. Musical notes often touches emotions so deep that words simply cannot reach.

If these songs are woven so inseparably into my faith, then surely I cannot help but sing them to others and teach them to a new generation of believers. We must sing, and bring hope through our song to all who hear.

Amen.

The Art And Agony Of Patience

My first child's due date was the week before Thanksgiving. In the early months of pregnancy, I imagined this date the doctor assigned to her to be a great blessing: a Thanksgiving baby! I actually envisioned having family around our home the entire holiday week — all there to welcome my baby. I could picture perfectly in my mind's eye this vision of everyone together, everyone happy, with food and the joy of saying our blessings out loud, creating the best possible environment for a new baby.

Of course, a due date is not a promise. A baby's due date is an educated guess, made by medical professionals with training and experience. They do not pick a date out of thin air, or with the assistance of a crystal ball. But even medical professionals realize that babies come in their own time.

I can remember having a conversation with a woman much wiser than myself during those early days of my first pregnancy. She asked me lots of questions about how I felt and what my experience with pregnancy had been, and my excitement to welcome a child into the world. When I told her my due date, I eagerly added my vision for Thanksgiving with family, all of us seated at a table and welcoming the newest little family member into the fold.

The woman's face suddenly changed. It was as if a warning bell went off in her mind, and her own experience as a mother compelled her to tell me some difficult truths. As gently as she could, she tried to lower my expectations for a *Norman Rockwell*-style Thanksgiving celebration, with a happy crowd and even happier newborn baby. She talked about the need for peace and rest.

But probably the most disconcerting advice she gave me was concerning the due date itself. "You know," I can remember her saying, "Children are like apples on an apple tree. They don't all fall on one day. Some fall ripe off the tree early, many will fall within a few days of each other, and some apples take a little bit more time to be ready."

The woman's words sounded like a lovely description of an apple tree, perhaps even a beautiful metaphor for pregnancy; but at the time, I simply nodded and decided to not pay this woman too much attention. Why stop the perfect holiday dream before it had even had a chance to arrive? I thought it was best to stick to my Thanksgiving baby plans. Somewhere, though, I tucked away these words of the woman's wisdom for later. Indeed, they would prove to be useful!

As November arrived, a different, more specific form of delivery date madness came to roost in my house. Now that Thanksgiving was closer, people around me began to speculate about the exact date of my daughter's birth.

"Perhaps she will arrive on my birthday!" an uncle exclaimed. "Maybe you could name her after me?!"

His comment seemed to set off a family game of calendar bingo: "Your great aunt's birthday was November 22!" "My brother's wedding anniversary is December 1!" "Wasn't our first Thanksgiving in this house on November 27?"

In addition to the pleas for particular dates, there were also what I termed the "woes": "Uncle George died on December 2." "I hope your baby doesn't arrive December 6; that was my ex-wife's birthday." And the general, "Try to avoid a holiday weekend when your regular doctor might be on vacation."

I understand that these comments were made as part of the give and take of conversation. But as November crept on, and my daughter's due date came and went, the comments only enforced the strange idea that the uncontrollable could be controlled, and, in turn, that I could and somehow should control such uncontrollable factors in life.

Needless to say, Thanksgiving was not as I had planned it to be. Neither was my daughter's arrival. She was born the first week in December, not as planned, but just as she was meant to be.

I wish I could say that I patiently waited for childbirth to happen. I wish I could say that my patience reduced my anxiety and made the whole birthing experience easy. I wish I could say I had any patience at all those weeks before and immediately after the due date! Instead, I found that not being able to control the timing of her arrival, not being able to control what turned out to be the beautiful arrival of new life, not being able to control all that was beyond my control left patience looking like an impossible ask.

I know — I need to have more patience. *I know*, I say to myself as I read these words from the New Testament book of James — I hear you speaking to me when you urge us all to be patient. I know — patience is exactly what I need and exactly what would provide me a proper frame of mind to face the challenges of each day. I know that I even desire patience as a necessary ingredient for my life's best recipe. And yet, patience can be elusive — especially, it seems, when we need it the most.

"Be patient," the author of James wrote, "until the coming of the Lord."

James' words have a particular context. If we understand James to be written in the earliest days of the Christian church, then the lens of suffering through which James wrote makes sense. The listeners who are the target audience of James' letter have been persecuted, scattered, shunned for what they believe — or, more exactly, in whom they believe.

When James talks about the coming of the Lord, readers have to believe that the Lord's arrival would be soon. Perhaps the example of the farmer guides us in our sense of time. Just as a farmer plants and can only hope for rain to come in due time and a crop to be produced, so we, too, are to hope, trust, and know that what has been planted will lead to a bountiful harvest.

Knowing that this result will come is to give us a confidence that leads to calm. We can strengthen our hearts. We can stop grumbling against one another. We can endure the suffering that comes at this time because we know that suffering will not last forever.

And yet... And yet, we in the present are still waiting for the coming of the Lord, just as James' audience also waited eagerly for his return. Advent is this incredibly strange and wonderful confluence of time where we prepare to celebrate the birth of a baby in Bethlehem, while also preparing for our Savior's return. Past and future make this present rich with meaning, and give a depth and necessity of patience to our everyday wondering and waiting.

Perhaps it is impossible to imagine what patience meant to the early church to whom James wrote, who were desperate to be set free from oppression, have their wrongs righted, and have their suffering relieved. Perhaps it is impossible to imagine what patience meant to an expectant Mary, visited by angels and traveling with her husband to Bethlehem under the weight of an emperor's census and all the hope of an entire people. Perhaps it is impossible to imagine patience in any sense other than the sensation of the years, days, hours, and moments that stretch out before us and demand our attention.

Patience is often spoken of as a gift that falls from the sky or is pulled out from a deep hidden reservoir within ourselves. But patience is never a virtue in a vacuum. It is always called upon in times of great distress; it is always needed most when strong forces are pulling at us from every side. Patience, therefore, is an essential part of every laboring process, as that upon which we place our ultimate hopes, comes into the fullness of life.

Of course, while reflecting on these loftier notions of patience, I am keenly aware that our world is eagerly anticipating the arrival of December 25. How do we wait? How do we help other people wait? And how do we articulate what it is exactly for which we are waiting?

If you have small children in your home, these loftier ideas of patience have already been dismantled by the arrival of excessive gift wish lists, holiday parties and pageants, plus general sugar-fueled Santa insanity that overtakes shopping centers and schools and seeps into the privacy of our homes as well.

In other words, urging patience to a seven-year-old at this time of year can be a grand adventure!

In many families, we exercise patience during this season in practical ways. Often holiday traditions help count the days, such as an Advent paper chain, traditions like baking cookies, or decorating the tree.

Many families also use an Advent calendar. Advent calendars give structure to what seems like such an unending wait, and an end date to the desired outcome. You might have grown up with an Advent calendar that was used in your family each year, highlighting biblical verses to tell the story of Advent and Christmas. Or you might cherish memories of a handcrafted calendar that beautiful told the story of the season through the arts.

In my home, we have often been drawn to the reward-based calendars that offer up a small decoration, chocolate every day, or even a small set of building blocks to create a toy. These were all great ideas but often seemed to push against the finer points of patience's art, as chocolates magically disappeared days in advance, the paper doors carefully reclosed as to appear they had never been opened... Who said my children could not be careful? For me, though, the Advent calendar that was most effective was the one that encouraged me to do something every day during the season. One day, for example, it instructed me to call a friend who lived far away. Another day meant reaching out to the neighbor across the street whose name I still did not know. Working with my children to gather clothes to donate occupied another day of waiting, while cans of food came with us to church on one of the Sundays.

Some other activities grew without the nudging of the calendar. We had made so many cookies that we should really share them with others, my daughter said while staring at a countertop full of holiday goodies. And donating one toy seemed small compared to all the toys my children had remembered receiving in years past.

None of the activities in the calendar were grand or difficult. In fact, many of them we had done before, and knew we should do them again. But it helped to be reminded that these little activities mattered; it helped each one of us to work together during a season where our patience seemed to be in short supply.

I do not know if these Advent-calendar-endorsed activities produced patience, but they did make the season brighter.

"Be patient, beloved." Jesus is coming. Our Savior is soon to arrive! Christmas is set on our calendars; our countdowns are marked. And yet the wait seems unending, and the timing of our Lord's coming uncertain.

This is a time we cannot force to come. This is a time we cannot control.

But we wait, because we proclaim together that this season of Advent has great meaning, and that together we hold patience until Christ comes again.

Amen.

A Gift With YOUR Name On It

As Christmas inches closer, the excitement level seems to reach higher and higher each day. In a household with young children, the excitement level seems to inch higher and higher every minute!

I grew up in a large family, as one of six children. Having six children in a house during the days leading up to Christmas meant an ever-growing level of chaos that seemed nearly impossible to contain! I remember lying awake in my bed at night, too excited to sleep, imagining what particular joys the upcoming Christmas festivities would bring. Of course, my joy at that age was solely concentrated on what gifts I would soon be opening.

One of the ways of monitoring the nearness of Christmas was to gauge the height of the wrapped presents that piled up underneath our Christmas tree. The tree was always in a corner of our living room, and beginning about a week before the day itself, gifts would begin appearing underneath the tree's bottom branches.

Some presents were dropped off by friends and neighbors. Some arrived in the mail. Some came home from school and church — little gifts from teachers we were to wait until Christmas to open. Each one got added to the pile, which grew and wrapped itself around the tree. We kids would rearrange the gifts into our own little piles and dream of what might be inside the pretty paper, underneath the bows, and inside the variety of boxes.

We kids also dreamed out loud about what gifts still might be coming our way. We wondered if a certain toy could possibly be in a box that size and shape, or if it was still to come…

The focus on our gifts became so all-consuming, in fact, that my mother tried to distract us. When games and songs and the light-hearted threat did not work to move us away from staring at the gifts under the tree, she instead came up with a genius idea. Rather than have name tags on all the presents so that we knew to whom the presents were given, she replaced all the name tags with a color-coded system, so that one child had gifts with a blue tag, one with a red tag, and so on.

The idea was that this way my mother could keep track of who got what gifts, but the kids would not know, and therefore we could not obsess over our gifts like a hawk eyeing its prey.

This was a great idea — it worked! While we kids spent lots of time shaking gifts, sizing them up, and guessing about their contents, we could never be absolutely certain which gifts belonged to each one of us.

There was just one problem. Perhaps you remember from the beginning of this story that I am one of six children? As you can imagine, this meant my mother's life was just a wee bit busy in the days leading up to Christmas.

So perhaps it was no surprise that when Christmas Eve rolled around, my mother could not find her list on which she had written out the color code for the presents, and could not remember which color of gift tag had been assigned to which child.

Let's just say the wrapping paper was flying especially fast that year as it was ripped off of gifts and thrown to the side! Luckily, the joy of presents greatly outweighed any confusion of the moment, so that even the chaos of opening all those gifts and figuring out who got what was still happy.

Perhaps name tags on gifts were not so important when I was a child, but names certainly are important. Regardless of age, we want to be known for who we are; we want to be recognized by name and be assured that our contribution to the world matters.

We have each experienced the discomfort of being unable to remember a person's name. We have each experienced the discomfort of having someone else be unable to remember our own name.

Every time, being unable to say the person's name out loud at an important moment brings a feeling of missed opportunity, loss, even disappointment. I wish I were able to recall names with ease, and could easily say the name of a person in order to add to the power of an encounter.

On the other side of the name game are the joyous times I have said names out loud in particular moments. "James, do you take Carolyn to be your wife?" "Amanda Jane, I baptize you in the name of the Father, and of the Son, and of the Holy Spirit." "Howard Michael, child of God, your sins are forgiven."

To say our particular names out loud is to acknowledge that the person in front of us is seen, and known — that we remember and proclaim their story, their gifts, and, ultimately, their relationship to God.

Paul's letter to the Romans began in a fashion that would be familiar to his original audience. Foregoing any suspense at the author, the letter did not save the signature for the end, but revealed the author's name at the very opening: "Paul, a servant of Jesus Christ, called to be an apostle, set apart for the gospel of God..." There was to be no mistaking that the author of this message was Paul himself.

But Paul's identity was not simply in his name. As he addressed the Christian community in Rome, he was quick to identify himself as first and foremost "a servant of Jesus Christ." Service was both his work and how he defined himself. Furthermore, his calling was that of an apostle — someone set apart and sent out to share the gospel with the world.

Who Paul was related to his authority. His apostle status was therefore integral to why he was the one writing this letter to the Romans. The gospel of God infused Paul's mission, his identity, his work, and his writing every day. It is because of the gospel that Paul's words to the Romans had power to move and shape them as a community of Christians.

With this authority, Paul immediately turned his letter's attention to the source and goal of his writing: Jesus Christ. The gospel proclaimed Jesus Christ, who, Paul told us, descended-from David, but was also the Son of God. His resurrection from the dead, his holiness and connection to God the Father was declared by Paul in those early verses. In other words, Paul wasted no time in reminding the Romans who Jesus was and how he was at the forefront of everything Paul said and did for the church.

Next came what Jesus continued to do — even after death and resurrection. Jesus Christ brings "grace and apostleship," resulting in faith for all people. Paul's description of Jesus was an active one — still bringing people to apostleship in an ever-expanding church. This circle of faith included Gentiles, including "all God's beloved in Rome, who are called to be saints."

By specifically naming the Romans as "God's beloved" and calling them "saints," Paul lifted up the Roman community for the message to come in the rest of the letter. Imagine these first verses as a name tag on an incredible gift — addressed directly to the people of the Roman church, who were called to work with Paul in the gospel of Jesus Christ. Grace and peace were theirs, given directly from "God our Father and the Lord Jesus Christ." With Jesus' name upon us, we are all granted the abundance of God's gifts.

So what gift would you like to receive this Christmas? Have you made your list? Have you checked it twice? Are you sure you know what would make the best addition to this year's Christmas gift exchange extravaganza?

Because there is a gift under the tree for us already. It is made just for us, and sits waiting with our name on it. In reading these words from Romans, Paul's words come to us, and the gifts of God's grace and peace are ours as well. Even when it is hard for us to believe the gifts are really meant for us, with our name written brightly on the tag.

One of the problems in hearing a beautiful passage like these words from Romans is that we get lost in the language, and can even forget to look for our name amongst all the gifts piled up by our Creator. Perhaps we do not even believe that we might receive, in addition to giving during this holiday time.

Take a moment in this busy season to name out loud the gifts you are receiving. What does grace look like? Where do you find peace? How does faith show up during this time in our lives?

One of the Advent gifts given to congregations is that of a Christmas pageant. Perhaps this Sunday is your church's pageant; perhaps you have vivid memories from pageants past.

I remember a parishioner once joking with me about what could possibly be new or different in the Christmas pageant this year — isn't it always the same story? "Yes," I would answer, "same story." And yet, the story is different every time when a young person claims it, proclaims it, and we dare to listen.

We vividly recall children dressed as sheep and shepherds, angels who cannot seem to stand still, baby dolls that are dropped, unscripted interludes that delight us and remind us of the pure joy of children.

We also vividly recall the singular power of a child's voice speaking the words of an angel. Our hearts swell as the simple songs of youth grow louder and declare "Away in a Manger." We find ourselves tearing up as a new crowd of children gather in awe around the baby. The message is powerful truth, even when the words seem a bit too large for the voices to which they have been assigned.

The truth is that we are changed when we hear the gifts of God proclaimed by a new voice. It is as if, in hearing an ancient story out of a young mouth, the gift is given all over again. We remember how precious and beautiful faith is, how grace comes as holy surprise, how God's peace defies silence and breaks bonds we think are unbreakable.

And in that moment, the gifts of God are given to us once again.

God's gifts do come anew to each generation, from Paul and the early church through every group of disciples who dared to gather in Christ's name and proclaim the good news in their own time. And in each new generation, these gifts insist on coming up close, being born into our very world, and daring to say our particular names out loud.

The truth is that the gifts Paul described in his letter to the Romans continue — even today. They are not limited by time or place, education or religious expertise. They are gifts of cosmic proportions that are simply unstoppable! They are also gifts that we know and can name personally.

The baby about to be born will change the world! And he will continue to change our lives, too.

Amen.

Nativity of the Lord
Titus 2:11-14

An Up-Close Nativity

One of my favorite childhood memories of Christmas is the decorations. Growing up, about mid-December, all these special decorations would come out of boxes and appear around the house. Ornaments for the trees, stockings for the mantle above the fireplace, pretty snow globes that sat on top of the bookshelves, and my mother's nativity scenes.

My mother owns several nativity scenes. They come in different sizes, are made of different materials, and show different interpretations of what the holy family looks like. They also display a lifetime of faith — of gifts that were given and received, relationships and friendships between giver and recipient.

Each scene tells a story — not only the story of the first Christmas echoing through the centuries, but of the artist who created the scene in their own eyes. The scenes tell the story of what my family looked like at different stages, too. More elaborate and intricate figurines indicate fewer young children were around to grab and break the pieces; more artistic versions show an emphasis trying to be taught, or a particular mission sweeping through the church at the time.

When I remember my mother's collection, the nativity scene most clearly detailed in my mind was made of glass — tiny etched figurines of Mary, Joseph, and baby Jesus, who rested on an intricate little manger. It was beautiful. And I remember that once we took it out of the box, it went high up on a shelf, so that little hands could not get to it.

But we could look at it, there up high in its spot. It was so perfect — and because of the way it was set aside and out of our reach, I knew that it had to be special, too.

Each and every nativity scene, it seems, grows in meaning as it becomes part of the owner's family. Each Christmas story, it seems, grows in depth to include us and speak to us in new ways.

My daughter's birthday is in early December, and when she was born, someone gave us a nativity scene to use in our home. It was beautiful, but it was created for a child: little plastic figures that gathered near a stable made of plastic and cardboard. The figures were short and stubby so that little hands could move them, and the stable had a button that, if pushed, would play "Hark the Herald Angels Sing."

Over many seasons, I have heard that button pushed many times, until the battery wore out. I still haven't replaced it — sorry.

The first few years we had that nativity set, I would place the figures in the places I had been taught to place them from my own childhood: Baby Jesus in the middle, Mary and Joseph right there alongside him, the angel up high in his own little designated nook, and animals scattered on the outside periphery with the shepherds.

But as my daughter and then son got older, they started to play with the scene and move the characters around. That was fine — although I did find myself sometimes putting everyone back in the spots I had picked out myself once my children were done playing and not paying attention.

Then something else happened. Somehow, as my children played, some of their other toys crept into the nativity scene. It didn't take long before stuffed animals, superheroes, dolls, and figurines of all shapes and sizes were flocking to the stable, and were all gathered around the manger and the baby Jesus.

A toy soldier stood at attention. A soft fabric doll loomed large over the angel. A caped action hero peered down to see what the animals also saw. A giant stuffed sheep mixed in with the plastic sheep that were sized to match the scenery.

Toys would appear, and then disappear. They would be moved, knocked down, and take the place of other figures, only to be moved again the next day. The scene would get crowded near the baby, while also expanding to include more and more figures each day, many of them looking quite out of place, until they were also moved. I wondered if they should go back to their previous spots.

These expanding and ever-changing nativity scenes were odd to see at first. It took more restraint than you can imagine not to "clean up" the scene and put everyone back where they, in my opinion, belonged! But it was also clear that my children understood the Christmas story better than I did.

"The grace of God has appeared, bringing salvation to all."

The book of Titus is a letter written by Saint Paul to his friend and mentee, Titus. Paul writes both about and to a young church that is growing into its own, and a young apostle eager to preach the gospel. As a Christian community, they are longing to tell others about the grace of God that has already appeared in Jesus Christ. They are also longing for the "blessed hope" that would appear when Christ comes again.

As Paul writes to Titus, the importance of the time in which they find themselves is always part of the story. There is an urgency to the message and an added importance to the community's actions in how they live out the message. Salvation is in their midst, and they are called to therefore take full advantage of this moment God has given them.

Why is this a passage of scripture we read at Christmas? Yes, salvation has appeared once again in the birth of Christ. And yes, we are called to fully awaken to the urgency of this moment in all its fullness. There is a very particular gift of time that is evident in Paul's words — time that seems to be both stand still enough to create sacred space in our midst, and time that pulls us ever forward, calling us to proclaim good news to the world.

The moment of Paul's letter to Titus is really the same conjunction of time in which we still find ourselves today. Past, present, and future all bear their weight on this day, and in many and various ways, we are able to recognize the particular timing of Christmas. The rush of the season pushes us too quickly, while loneliness and grief can make the moments unbearably heavy on our hearts. We hold memories of gifts from our childhood

— even smells and the tastes of old family recipe that only a relative could make perfectly. We long for a Christmas when all people will come together, when all will not want for anything, and when peace will reign.

Past, present, and future seem like too much for any one day to hold. And perhaps Christmas cannot hold it all perfectly still, in silhouette for us to view from afar.

No — Christmas is not only a capsule of nostalgia, meant to dwell on the good old days of Christmases past. As Christians, we celebrate Christmas because of the hope it brings for Christ's return to Earth — a hope born in our midst again this very moment.

This movement of Christmas calls to us — not only to observe, but to join in both the celebration and the work ahead.

Are we open to the gift of salvation right in front of us? Are we willing to get up close and see it? Are we able to let it move and change us? Or have we put Christmas up on a shelf, so precious that we fear it might break if we get too close to it?

Nativity scenes can say an awful lot about our faith. They can be stunningly beautiful — an absolute gift from God — but sometimes so precious to us that we consider them fragile, too. We might be tempted to put them far away, out of reach of little hands — or even behind glass, locked up, and out of reach for any of us to actually touch and move.

We have in our minds the places where each character in the story of Christmas is supposed to stand and not move — the shepherds always standing sentry, the animals quiet and subdued, the parents of the baby protective, the baby himself never crying. The characters are supposed to stay still — never moving, never breaking.

We have in our minds the places of how and where faith is supposed to go, too. We determine, in theory, what our faith is supposed to look like, where the characters stand in relation to one another, how they form a scene that will look perfectly beautiful to the eye.

Each of us has imagined the rites of passage that mark our faith journeys and life achievements: baptism, Holy Communion, education, love and the expansion of our own families, work, pleasure, and personal growth.

And often the models in our minds look nothing like real life, and nothing like our own lives, either. We can spend lots of time trying to rearrange things to the way they used to be, the way we imagine they are supposed to be. We can exhaust ourselves simply wishing that the world would stop changing all around us and knocking the scene out of place.

Maybe we don't even bring out the nativity scene anymore — if we think it too childish, or too much a relic of our past.

This year, I want to invite you to be part of the nativity scene, too. Imagine that this scene is not just something to look at, but a story that invites you to join in. Imagine that you are asked to get a little closer, to see the baby in the manger. Imagine that you belong in that scene, right alongside the shepherds and angels, the sheep and donkey. Imagine that you bring something unique to the story to enrich it — that you need to be up close, and to see the gift coming into the world tonight.

Because we do not worship a God who stays high and far away, and watches from the top shelf. No, we worship — we proclaim — a God who chose to come right here into our world — to be born in a shape like ours — to feel highs and lows like we do — in order to draw us close: to a manger, to a cross, to light and love as only God can give.

On this eve of Christmas, we listen, and we proclaim that a Savior has been born to us — called Immanuel, which means *God with us*. The divine, literally *in the flesh* — coming into this world in the most fragile form we can imagine — a tiny newborn baby, surrounded by poor traveling parents, working animals, and shepherds from the hillside.

Angels announce this child's birth. And they call to each of us to join in the singing and gather around, alongside the shepherds and animals and holy family. You are welcome here — the rich and poor, the fragile and strong; those who know their way around the stable, and those for whom this is all new.

There's always room for one more in this nativity scene set before us on Christmas Eve — there's always a way for it to grow and include each and every one us. My children had to teach me that. That we each need to get close, so that we each might also truly witness that Christ is born.

Christmas has come again, my friends. The world — and our lives — can never be the same again.

Amen.

To Tell The Story Again

When my children were little, I was eager to show them Christmas in interactive and fun ways. I also think I was eager to share with them the Christmas joy that children possess and are so eager to pass on to others.

During one Christmas season, my husband and I took our young family to an outdoor Christmas market in Philadelphia that is well known for its beautiful crafts and holiday foods. This particular market is also well known for its location — right in the heart of the city.

The hype we had heard was accurate. The goods for purchase were handcrafted and beautiful, the food delicious, the atmosphere festive. There were actually chestnuts roasting on an open fire! I remember the sights, sounds, and smells of the market were wonderful, and I felt like I was living my ideal Christmas.

But as we stayed and continued to walk around the area surrounding the market, the festive Christmas veneer started to wear off; the realities of city life, especially city life in the winter, became clearer. Folks were sleeping on cardboard near the sidewalk vents, huddled in layer upon layer of clothing and blankets. Signs asking for monetary help were accompanied by the occasional loud shout that was unfamiliar to young ears. And as we tried to leave a busy parking garage, the honks of traffic and the smell of exhaust not only suggested city congestion, but an overwhelming congestion of all of our senses.

In other words, the glitz and glam of the Christmas market were only part of the Christmas story of the city.

As we drove back home, I answered questions from my children in rapid succession: *Why are people asking for money? Doesn't everyone have a house? Why was daddy honking so much? Where is that lady's Christmas tree, and how does Santa get gifts to her?* I pondered my own questions about the day we had just experienced, too, including, *How much should I tell my children, and how much should I keep to myself?*

The truth was that I did not have easy answers to any of my children's questions — nor to my own that day. But I also had a strong sense that our experience was still very much Christmas — all the sights, all the smells, all the sounds, all the questions. Somehow — for all of us — including every soul we had encountered that day — Christmas had come, and the gift of a Savior was given to us all.

Christmas is often remembered by me for what I consider its fragile moments of beauty: the quaintness of the manger, the warmth of family and friends around a table, the glow of small candles lighting up faces while "Silent Night" is sung *a capella*. Those memories are beautiful. And I guess I have made these memories so precious that I am afraid they will get broken in the reality of the rest of the year.

We know that it doesn't take long for the news headlines to sing in the background of our Christmas carols. Cries of hunger, the vast chasm between the rich and poor, political insults, mass shootings, drumbeats of war, anger and fear of all the "others" — bad news does not take a Christmas vacation.

I wonder why my instinct is to protect Christmas — to imagine it as breakable as a hand-blown glass ornament, or as prone to flying away as tinsel? Why do I imagine Christmas to be as rare and precious as the few snowflakes my children have seen since our climate has warmed? Where does it come from — my need to keep Christmas neat and clean, precious and up on a shelf, far removed from the inescapable sin and brokenness of our world?

It was only a few days ago we gathered here in our sanctuary with warmth and hope, and held our precious little candles as we sang "Silent Night." It was only a few days ago that gifts sat perfectly wrapped under our trees, and were quickly opened by joyous faces. It was only a few days ago that we celebrated the birth of our Savior: a baby born in Bethlehem. It was only a few days ago that all seemed good and holy and right.

But even the story on Christmas hinted at the political forces at work during Jesus' birth: a census ordered by the Roman empire, which put Mary and Joseph on the move to Bethlehem. And when there was no room for them in the inn, their baby was welcomed in a stable and slept in a manger.

Usually we view the details of the stable animals and the manger as cute and charming in the Christmas story, but they also tell the story of how God shows up amongst the poor and humble.

Today, the story continues. We often don't read this gospel from Matthew, but it is traditionally told as part of the twelve days of Christmas. And after hearing it, it's a story we would probably rather forget.

It seems that Jesus' birth was not welcomed by all. When King Herod heard the news of Christmas, he began a search for the child born in Bethlehem, to destroy him. But a dream warned Joseph to flee the coming destruction, and the holy family escaped to Egypt, and then later to Nazareth.

The poor family staying with animals in Bethlehem was now a refugee family fleeing death and destruction — saved by a dream, and by a father's willingness to travel to a foreign land and depend on the hospitality of others in order to preserve the life of his child.

The other children of Bethlehem who did not flee were not so fortunate. Another name for this First Sunday after Christmas is the Slaughtering of the Innocents, and there is little sense that can be made of it. Innocent children — who had the misfortune of being born in the same town as Jesus — are killed *en masse* at the hands of King Herod's military. Why? Simply because Herod was afraid of losing his power.

It sounds absurd: for a man in a palace with his own army to be threatened by poor children under the age of two. And yet, history is full of stories of the powerful threatened by those on the margins.

So why tell such an awful story of human brutality so close to the beautiful story of Christ's birth? Because, as our epistle from Hebrews reminds us, it is precisely into such a broken and brutal world that Christ was born.

"For it is clear that he did not come to help angels, but the descendants of Abraham," (verse 16).

Jesus was fully human, born into a life that knew suffering, even suffering endured in his infancy. It is through this suffering, and, ultimately, through his death, that Jesus conquered sin and death and became a beacon of grace, mercy, and the fullness of life.

I realize we probably are still reluctant to hear such trage-dies as the fate of the innocent children of Bethlehem in the glow of Christmas. I realize Good Friday seems far away from our minds. I admit my own reluctance to preach — even to read — any story with shades of suffering and death when the world is still hoping to eke out a few more moments of Christmas hope before going back to our working routine.

These stories of the First Sunday in Christmas are too de-pressing. They are too close to Christmas and too confusing — too timely. They feel too similar to the political fights we are em-broiled in over power and greed and fear— which seem to have been political fights since the days of King Herod.

So why preach them? Because we must. Because once these stories are told out loud, they cannot be ignored.

There are still too many poor families on the run; too many women, like Rachel, who wail for the loss of their children at the hands of violence. There are still too many of our leaders who are thirsty for power. There is still suffering, and there are still too many of us who try to drown out cries of injustice with shal-low songs of the season.

There are still too many of us who have learned to look the other way.

Christmas didn't make all the bad news go away. But the birth of our Savior does give us good news, too — good news that is born at the very heart of all that is scary and dark. Good news that demands that we listen, and that we take it seriously.

Our gospel today makes it clear that if you are looking for God, you will not find him in a palace, or at the head seat of an empire. No, you will find God on the margins — born in a stable, fleeing with the persecuted, wherever people are hurting. Throughout the Christmas season, we are reminded that God enters fully into our suffering in order that all might have life.

That means none of us are forgotten. And all of us are needed to keep telling the story, and share what we have learned about the Savior who came for all of us.

Amen.

A Vision Of Now

I will be healthier.
I will eat more vegetables, including the green ones.
I will spend more time with my family.
I will shop locally.
I will be more patient — with my family.
I will be more patient — with myself.
I will spend less time on the internet… and on the couch….
And on the couch surfing the internet…

Some are generic, some are specific, most are well-intentioned, few are achievable.

Yes, it is the time of year for New Year's resolutions. It is the time to consider where life has taken us, where we are now, and where we want to go. A moment to intentionally pause and evaluate what we want to make of this time we have on Earth and the gifts with which we have been blessed.

Or, if that sounds way too serious and intense, perhaps we can each simply take a moment to open our eyes to what is right in front of us now.

We recently hosted a concert at my church. I was not one of the performers, but simply the hostess. Hours before the performance began, I worked my way through a mental to-do list:

1. Unlock all the doors (which we all know involves an insane amount of doors and an even more insane amount of thought as to which doors to unlock for any church building).
2. Check the thermostat and see if the temperature was set to the right digits and had not been adjusted by someone else.

3. Check the sign outside to make sure it was advertising the concert.
4. Test the sidewalks for slippery spots and debris.
5. Bring out the programs for the evening and set them on the usher table.
6. Take a peek at the bathrooms to make sure they are ready for the evening ahead.
7. Turn on all the lights in the sanctuary.
8. Check the temperature in the sanctuary (again) to see if the thermostat is actually working.

It was then, on a routine check of the sanctuary at the conclusion of my to-do list, that I noticed a quiet figure sitting in one of the pews. I couldn't tell if the person was praying, or just sitting — if they were innocent or to be treated as a threat. But as I got closer, my internal questions were cut short by the person's comment.

"These stained glass windows are gorgeous," the man said. I nodded as the man continued. "I came here early for the concert so I could sit here and look at the windows in the changing light. That's how I remember your church — the one with the stained glass windows. I could spend hours in here, just looking at the light coming through there."

I nodded again in agreement, and said something generic about thanking him for attending our concert that evening.

"Do you know what the windows mean?" he asked me.

Oh — good question, I thought to myself. "We have a brochure in the back," I answered, and offered to go get one for the man.

He thanked me, and read the brochure in the time waiting for the concert to begin. But the man's attention was not captured by the brochure. Instead, he mostly just looked at the colorful pieces of glass embedded in the brick wall that somehow, together, created a beautiful display of light.

The truth is, I did not know the meaning of the windows. I had looked at them many times — meaning that I had passed by them and glanced at them while walking around the sanctuary setting up, cleaning up, or doing something that seemed very important in that moment. I believe once I had even caught a glimpse of the reflected colors of light on the wall of the sanctuary. I had noted that the colors were interesting, even curious in how they moved about and scattered. But even after noting their beauty, I had kept walking, kept looking ahead, kept moving my line of sight, kept on going about my business.

The windows do have official interpretations — the stories outlined in the brochure I had given to the visiting man. They offered a good explanation of the biblical stories that inspired the windows, including the way they told a continuing story if you walked in a particular direction around the building. But the true beauty of the windows was in the light of the moment and place — how it looked, even how it felt, to be sitting right there where you were — and to watch the light shine through.

I want to invite us all to sit for a moment. I want to invite us to watch the light of right here and now shimmering all around us — the light reflected through the vision of John of Patmos. It is, not mildly put, a revelation — a vision from God — a divine dance of colors moving in unison while playing with harmonies in a wholly new way.

John declared that he had seen a "new heaven and a new earth... the new Jerusalem." The vision was enough to take one's breath away, just like a woman who was transformed into the particular beauty of a bride meeting her bridegroom. The ancient city of Jerusalem, along with all of heaven and earth, were made new.

John's revelation, even reflected through centuries of history and the translation of words into our own language, still takes our breath away. Imagine how beautiful the vision was to John when he first beheld its glory!

One particular aspect of the revelation's beauty is what is not said. While John's words are descriptive, their power is in their ability to invoke our own particular memories and dreams of beauty. Imagine, the words invite, the most beautiful bride you have ever seen walking down the aisle. Imagine, indeed, the city we know and love now transformed into its new self, all of its flaws perfected, all of its particular highlights accentuated. Imagine a place where our tears are being wiped away by our Creator, and the grief and pain that have become so normal to us in this lifetime, no longer exist.

It is a vision both familiar and beyond our own imaginations. At the same time, we not only are astounded by newness, but challenged to let go of burdens we have carried for so long that we find it difficult to imagine life without them.

Only God has the power to create such a vision for us. "The one seated on the throne... [is] mak[ing] all things new," John tells us. He is the "Alpha and the Omega, the beginning and the end." If this is so, then God holds all of time — including all of our time — in his hands.

It is the time for New Year's resolutions. Have you made yours yet? Did you begin action on them today? Did you already fail in their execution? Did you not bother with creating resolutions, since you anticipated their failure before you even began with a new year?

Sometimes I wonder if I am able to dream of new things for myself. Even as I open a new calendar to hang on the wall, even as I look at an empty slate of possibilities, I worry that the past has already filled my calendar for the new year.

Our reading from Revelation reflects light on our today, and offers us a path forward.

So how will we even begin to imagine God making all things new?

When John of Patmos received the revelation from God, he was imprisoned and punished for his faith. John knew well the limitations of his dwelling place and his situation in life, and he had every reason to be confined to the limits fear puts on our lives.

And yet God burst through the walls of John's imprisonment. Indeed, God had already dreamed a future for him and for all humanity, offering a vision of newness that encompassed past and future to paint the present in a new way. This revelation is so imprinted on John that he must share it with the world.

I wonder how God can break us out of our limitations. Are we able to let our past mistakes and failures not limit our future dreams? Can we embrace a vision of new life that God offers us? Do we make space for new possibilities? Or do we fall back into our old habits, our old ways, our old routines, our old… everything, even the things we do not like and wish we could change?

As I start a new year in my congregation, I am vowing to make time to watch the light that comes in through the stained glass windows in the sanctuary. This has meant setting aside time, sitting still, and allowing spaces for quiet.

It has also meant setting aside what I thought I knew about these windows, or what I have been told they mean, in order to be open to the light coming through and shining near to me.

Although I have not had a vision like John of Patmos while watching the stained glass windows, the light has still surprised me. If you sit in the back of the sanctuary, the light from the top of the windows makes the colors look bright and bold, and you wonder how you did not notice it before. If you sit up close, the light is splintered all around you and seems to embrace your presence in its space.

In the morning, the windows look still as windows should be, while in the late afternoon they seem to come alive and be part of a larger show that seeks an audience. Even at night, when the spotlight shines in from outside, the windows still look alive with light, as if even the disappearance of the sun itself could not stop the colors of light from showing up in the sanctuary for all who are patient enough to wait and watch for them.

And if you sit to the side of the windows at just the right time, and the light is shining through the windows at just the right angle, the light does appear to dance. It moves up and down, grows bigger and smaller, even seems to dance to music only the light can hear. Or perhaps the light creates its own music.

It is a beautiful sight to behold, and it transforms the space that is so familiar into a new place beyond any one person's imagination. Indeed, only God can cast such a vision of dancing light.

God has a dream for us, a vision of a new heaven and a new earth that includes us, too. And even though it appears as the distant future, it works in and through all the broken pieces of this world, assembling them into a beautiful work of art through which light shines even more brilliantly.

We are invited to see this vision. We are welcomed into this moment when God's presence shines brightly for us to witness.

Amen.

True Riches Of Grace

My grandmother was of a generation that treasured dishes. I do not mean she treasured particular foods and protected family recipes, but rather that she treasured the plates and serving bowls that were used once upon a time to hold the food.

Like many women of her era, my grandmother stored her sentimental wealth in a large wooden hutch with glass doors that sat in her dining room. No matter where she lived, or how often she moved, the hutch always enjoyed a place of prominence, and never lost a single item within its valued stock.

If you had the time, or did not know any better, Grandma would be more than pleased to take you on a tour of that hutch. Indeed, each item had a story of its own, adding to the storied family legend of the hutch as a whole.

Displayed on the top shelf were the teacups my grandmother had collected on her travels around the world when she was younger and more adventurous, and when her knees did not ache too much. In one side compartment of the hutch was a decorative gold-trimmed shaving mug that had been left on the family farm by a bachelor uncle who was visiting during harvest season and never cared to retrieve the possession. On the opposite side, a plate that was clearly designed for a child, with sledding children dressed in their old-fashioned winter best — muffs and furs and all — displayed in the center of the plate. The letters of the alphabet were boldly printed all around the edge of this plate that was so delicate and fragile it seemed impossible to believe a child had ever touched it, let alone eaten off of its beautifully painted surface.

The dishes that had been used for years at Christmas and Thanksgiving were stored in the drawers underneath, their place out of the spotlight not due to their loss of beauty, but simply because my grandmother no longer hosted big family meals and had tucked these items in high-value storage. There were a few items my grandmother still used, scattered here and there on the other shelves behind glass, along with gifts she continued to receive from friends and inherit from deceased relatives.

In the central place of honor in the hutch was a serving bowl that's beauty was only matched by its story. The bowl was white with painted pink flowers. Gold accents marked its treasured status. But its real uniqueness, my grandmother said, was its scalloped edges. I could not ever imagine any food actually being served out of such an intricate and exotic bowl in the middle of the North Dakota prairie, but my grandmother assured me that was the case — mashed potatoes and all! And my grandmother was never wrong about such things, or so she told me.

The story goes that the bowl had originally belonged to my great grandmother — most certainly an item that was gifted, or pined after, and saved for over a long period of time. When my great grandmother had moved into a care facility near the end of her life, it was this bowl that she insisted move with her into her tiny clean room with the same white walls as every other room in the building. And it was this bowl that my grandmother had been carrying on an icy sidewalk on moving day when she had slipped, fallen, and somehow, most miraculously of all, caught in her arms as she was sprawled on the concrete — a falling, fragile time capsule whose safety seemed to bring some assurance to my great grandmother in her new stage of life.

In case you couldn't tell, I heard this story many times as a child and young adult. I had heard the story often enough not only to believe it, but to make it my own as I looked at that bowl in the hutch. It told a story of my family, and its unbroken existence seemed to prove something about my grandmother's strength as well.

My siblings heard all of these stories, too. We remember them differently, with various details added that match our personalities, interests, and personal relationships with Grandma. Sometimes when we were together in her tiny apartment with white walls, we would look at the dishes and say which ones were our favorites. Sometimes, when our mother was not around to chastise us, we would speculate on what we imagined to be the most valuable items in the collection.

As my grandmother aged, she began to worry that the stories behind each treasured item in her hutch might be lost, and so she created a coded system to categorize the items and link them to stories she had written and saved in a folder.

Grandma suspected, rightly, that her grandchildren probably were not listening as attentively as they should be to her stories. She was also disturbed by a friend who had told her that younger generations had lost interest in dishes, and that their monetary value had plunged in recent years. While the value outsiders placed on the items was not my grandmother's focus, she seemed quite sad in telling us that all antiques only have value relative to the owner. In other words, Grandma became deeply concerned that her dishes were only valuable to her alone.

My grandmother died during a brutally cold spell in February. Supposedly the weather was cold but fair for her funeral; I was stuck at O'Hare in an ice storm that kept me far from home. While I grieved her death and directed my anger at the airline, I also had to admit that such weather seemed like the setting of many of my grandmother's stories, and fit this final one, too.

It was not long after her funeral that talk turned to Grandma's dish hutch, and the need to move everything out of her apartment and offer the small apartment with still-white walls to someone new. What was fair in distributing the prized possessions was deemed to be that the oldest grandchild had first pick, and so on, down the line.

Since I could not make it out to point, bargain, and claim my favorite dish in person, I knew I had given up my spot in the pecking order. I did, however, make an effort to share with my sisters how much I had always admired the serving bowl with the pink flowers, gold accents, and fragile scalloped edges. I hoped for the best, but was only told my item could not be shipped, and I would have to pick it up myself.

I waited months until I could visit in person and pick up the item I was given during the family clean out.

My surprise in this story is not that the scallop-edged bowl now sits in my own dining room hutch. No, my great surprise was to see how the other items were claimed by family members. No one wanted the shaving mug; the alphabet plate sits in a drawer somewhere so as not to be broken by a family with small children. And in my youngest sister's hutch — displayed with prominence in her own dining room — is an item I had almost forgotten. But I remembered its provenance the second I set foot in my sister's house, with a story that did not need to be written down by my grandmother.

The precious item my sister chose is a light green plastic storage container, with a well-worn but still tight-fitting white lid. When I saw it in her home, I did not have to ask why she had chosen that particular dish. It does not have a long family history attached to it; it is not rare or of a high monetary value. No, it was the container my grandmother had used whenever she made "jello salad" — her own unique concoction that veered far from any traditional definition of salad.

Why choose a plastic container rather than an intricate porcelain bowl, or gold-trimmed mug? My sister's choice was made because it was the only item she had ever seen our grandmother actually use. It was the item that actually left the hutch on a regular basis, and the item that was not afraid to have children's hands touch it. It was the dish connected most deeply to my sister's own story — to her own memories of Grandma.

To my sister, that plastic container remains the most valuable item she could have chosen, and she treasures it still.

The passage from Ephesians on which we dwell today for God's Word is part of the letter's introduction. We hear of God's blessings for us — blessings that are not stingy, but "lavish." Through Christ, we have redemption, forgiveness, and the "riches of his grace."

The praise continues, as the author of Ephesians is awestruck to think of God's great gifts that are given freely to us by God through Jesus, the Beloved.

There is no indication in this passage that we have earned any of these gifts. Rather, it is God's "good pleasure" to bring us into these blessings, and for our "adoption as his children."

Much of the language in this passage is what might be termed "church language." We are accustomed to hearing about forgiveness and grace; perhaps we even take for granted the hope that these ancient words contain.

But to hear these words in the context of the ancient church is to revisit the experience of lavish blessings upon which this letter dwells. No longer was anyone to be a second-class citizen, or related to a lower status in society. No — to be adopted as God's children through Jesus Christ is to enjoy the fullness of blessings God offers to all.

Sometimes it is difficult for us to see the good gifts of God in front of us. We are dazzled by what the world considers valuable; we are prone to overlooking the enormous beauty of God's gifts to us that give life.

I wonder if this passage from Ephesians today might call us all into a new vision. With the blessings of God, we might be able to view one another not as competitors in the endless quest for value that this world sets before us, but to see all as brothers and sisters in Christ in this shared inheritance of God's grace.

Ephesians reminds us that, first and foremost, God sees value in us. We are each marked with the "seal of the promised Holy Spirit;" we are blessed beyond measure by this good news of God's unending grace.

Amen.

Epiphany of the Lord
Ephesians 3:1-12

The Puzzle Of God's Wisdom

Christmas vacation in my home while growing up involved lots of time with a jigsaw puzzle. Often the puzzle was a family gift given on Christmas Day. It was meant to give us something to do and perhaps even bring us closer as a family by working together on a common goal. At least, that was the hope.

Soon after ripping off the wrapping paper, the box would be opened and the contents would be spilled out on a card table in the living room, with everyone taking a hand in putting the pieces together to re-create the beautiful scene on the box cover.

The picture on the cover was always a "good one": something that looked lovely, would keep our interest, encourage conversation, and promised to be fun to solve. The picture on the cover was also almost always deceiving. When we started the project, we assumed it would be quick and easy; sometimes we even wondered what we would do with all of our extra time once the puzzle was completed.

After all, we were good at puzzles. We were smart, hard-working, and diligent in our approach. We had young eyes, quick fingers, and flexible necks not yet stiff with arthritis. With the right approach and the application of our superior problem-solving skill, no puzzle could stay in pieces for long.

Of course, the puzzles were never as easy as we dreamed them to be. We often struggled to find the right pieces at the right time, and our fighting over who was going to the border and complete it first probably did not help our ability to solve the puzzle either. We would drop pieces, forget the pieces we had been just recently looking at, and occasionally spitefully hide a piece here or there to enrage a particular sibling.

As we got older, the puzzles got harder: more pieces, smaller pieces, less color variation, harder to fit shapes. As we got older, our family got bigger, too, with younger siblings pulling up chairs to the puzzle table and "graduating" to the role of puzzle solver.

Now when I look at a puzzle box, I think about all the time and energy it will take to put it all together. I can very quickly and easily come up with a long list of reasons to not bother bringing the puzzle box down from the top closet shelf and opening the box. To begin solving such a puzzle always takes work.

But hopefully we have all experienced the job of solving a puzzle as well. Part of the joy is completing a long and grueling process. Part of the joy is simply making it to the end! But the greatest joy for me was always in somehow working together with family members to complete the project. When we set aside our differences, when we each did our part, when everyone contributed time, energy and skill to the shared goal, there was joy in the shared solution.

Indeed, there are few feelings as satisfying as looking at the empty puzzle box cover and seeing the picture match the completed puzzle on the table.

The word "mystery" appears several times in this week's lesson from Ephesians. Paul repeats saying "mystery" throughout the passage to such a degree that the text itself begins to seem obscure, with perhaps a hidden message.

But as Paul continues, he reveals that this mystery is related to Gentiles having access to the same gospel and the same promise in Christ as Jews. All are heirs and members of the same body, entitled to the same gift of grace.

Paul states that this mystery was revealed to him by revelation, and that it was not known to previous ancestors in the faith. However, rather than boast of this chosen status as one who received revelation from God, Paul reminds the reader he is a servant of the gospel and calls himself the "least of all the saints."

Once this mystery was known, Paul was eager to share its knowledge. He pronounces that such wisdom of God be shared through the church.

There is a beautiful turn of phrase here where Paul describes the wisdom of God "in its rich variety." In the context of what Paul has revealed about mystery, we can see rich variety in how both Jews and Gentiles share in the promise of Jesus Christ.

While the categories of Jews and Gentiles do not mark such a clear distinction or perhaps reflect the fullness of the great variety in today's world, we can add our own picture of what the "wisdom of God in its rich variety" might mean now.

We have witnessed the gospel of Jesus Christ reaching into far corners of the globe, the word of God being translated into a kaleidoscope of languages, cultures, and traditions, and the great beauty of how the grace of Christ can bring very different people together in a common mission of service.

Indeed, the call to love our neighbor provides a continuing challenge to reach across boundaries, leave our comfort zones, and listen to the voices of others who might be quite unlike ourselves. If we consider what this means in our daily lives, and for the life of our own congregations, it means work — often difficult work to try and intentionally seek and gather the rich variety of God's wisdom. And yet, these words of Ephesians remind us that the beautiful mysteries of God do not exist only for us, but call us to always keep asking who needs to hear the gospel next.

Now that I am an adult with a family of my own, I have several jigsaw puzzles in my hallway storage closet just waiting to be completed. Some are treasured puzzles my family has completed before; many of them are in boxes yet to be opened. To look at the picture on the cover of the box is lovely, but it is not the point of a puzzle.

No, a puzzle exists to challenge the mind and memory, the skills of our nimble fingers and our endurance and eyesight. Puzzles are mysteries waiting for us to open them, wrestle with them, discover their complexity as they come together. The more intricate and complicated the puzzle, the richer the enjoyment when the pieces take shape and the full picture can be seen.

Perhaps the same can be said in regard to our faith lives.

One of the reasons I love reading scripture is that even though these ancient words have been poured over and studied by millions of people over thousands of years, they still have mystery in them. They can speak to us in new ways, challenge us to see the world differently, challenge us to see ourselves differently. The same scripture passage I understood so well two years ago can be confounding now, while a passage I never understood as a child may now appear written directly to my heart.

One of the reasons I love being part of a church community is to worship together. I know — that sounds quite obvious. But it is actually both uplifting and challenging to pray with another, to sing with another, to sit with another. At any given worship service, I might know a majority of the folks by name in my little congregation, and yet I still do not often know why they are smiling or teary that morning, or simply what moved them to join the gathering in that place and time. The picture they present publicly might be just one angle of the fullness of their life.

One of the reasons I love Holy Communion is to hear proclaimed that I am part of the body of Christ — that God wants to be part of my life and who I am in my own unique and strangely wonderful ways. At the same time as I feel seen, I am also joined in this body of Christ with all the folks there with me. That means we have to work together to be eyes and ears, arms and feet, heart and head. We do not all agree on the hows and whats of mission, but we do agree on the why: that God has called us together by grace. I am therefore given an opportunity to join the body of Christ with the people all around me.

When we recite creeds together, when we visit the sick together, when we paint walls together and sit through long meetings together, we reflect the rich variety of God's wisdom. We might not think the pieces fit together too well, or that the picture is unclear, or that the work will never be completed. We wonder when we will ever find that last piece that completes the picture; we worry that the puzzle might be too hard for us to solve. But we keep trying, putting together one piece at a time.

We know and we believe that the Spirit is always moving, always revealing, always putting pieces together and then confounding us once again. We know and we believe that this complex mystery of creation that we are part of reflects the rich variety of God's wisdom.

It means I am called to see my brothers and sisters in Christ in a whole new way. Imagine if each challenging encounter with a person was guided by a question of how the person reflects the rich variety of God's wisdom. Imagine if our conversation was an opportunity for each of us to learn and view one another in a new light. Imagine if the people who I think are so different from myself — and so difficult to get along with — were actually pieces of a beautiful puzzle, just as I am. Imagine if the goal in meeting someone who challenged me was not to convince the person to be like me, but to imagine how we might together contribute to something larger than either of us alone.

God's mystery is just like that. Perhaps we can describe it as a jigsaw puzzle, ever growing more difficult and complicated to solve, and also growing more interesting, with interlocking parts and edges we never noticed before. It might never be solved by us, but God assures us that he holds the mystery in his hands, revealing it throughout time — revealing the truth of the gospel even in our time. Indeed, we are blessed to be part of this picture of God's wisdom, alive today.

Amen.

Baptism of the Lord / First Sunday after the Epiphany
Acts 10:34-43

God's Ever-Growing Community

Is there anyone more open-minded than me?

As a young pastor right out of seminary, I thought the answer was an emphatic "no!" I imagined myself to be at the cutting edge of theology, worship practice, and church administration, and an expert on all the current perplexing issues of the day. I also believed that my heart and eyes were absolutely wide open to where the Holy Spirit was moving in our midst.

It's probably no surprise to hear that leaving seminary and being called to serve in an actual church involved lots of reality checks — many of which meant I learned how little I knew about the many things I thought I knew well! I also witnessed how my own heart and mind needed to be opened.

Only a few months into my call, a young family showed up for worship. They sat in the back, observing the service, while patiently listening to every word spoken and sung, coordinating their own actions with all the standing, sitting, kneeling, and re-peat cycle that goes on during a regular weekly service in that particular congregation. After the service was over, they waited patiently for everyone to shake my hand and leave, and then asked to speak with me.

They told me their story — of recently arriving in the United States from India, of working in the computer industry, of their educational dreams for their young son, of their strong Christian faith. They wanted permission to come to church and worship with the congregation.

I remember responding in a verbal fashion that was similar to the physical sensation of jumping out of one's seat: "Yes! Of course you are welcome here! Please come and join us!" I also remember feeling a sort of euphoria that happens whenever visitors decide they want to keep coming to church, as if to shout out loud, "Wow! These folks really like us and are going to come back!"

In further interactions and conversations with the visitors, it became clear that they felt comfortable in our little church. They knew the same hymns, they followed along with the liturgy, and they paid close attention to the sermon and announcements. They genuinely wanted to be part of the church community. Frankly, it felt good to welcome them and experience the joy and energy they brought with them to praise God.

I tell the story of this family becoming part of the congregation because I am somewhat embarrassed that the story did stand out in my mind. I wish I could say that visitors were so numerous that this family was just one of hundreds participating in the life of the church. I wish I could say that the congregation was so accustomed to welcoming new people that I never gave it a second thought.

But we were a small, close-knit group. We all sort of knew each other's stories, and we all sort of expected certain behaviors and traditions from one another. So I guess there was part of me that was surprised at how easily this new family fit in with our congregation's customs and traditions. I was even more surprised at what happened the first time we all shared communion together.

This church took communion as a solemn rite and ritual. It was unusual to hear any chattering while people waited their turn to come up to the altar rail that separated the front of the church from the pews. Worshipers would kneel and pray while waiting their turn, and would often remain kneeling at the rail in prayer even after they had received bread and wine and a blessing.

Our newest visitors did not seem daunted at all by the communion ritual, showing their comfort around what can seem like a highly choreographed dance routine for people who have never participated before. Not only were they calm and collected, but they were true to themselves and remembered what was an integral part of communion for them. As they prepared for receiving the holy elements, they added their own important custom and solemnity to the ritual: they walked up to the front of the church, carefully removed their shoes, and placed their footwear gently and silently to the side of the aisle before kneeling in prayer.

It was obvious that removing their shoes was a sign of respect for the sacrament. And yet, I remember being worried that some of the more traditional members of the congregation might object to seeing people remove their shoes and exposing their bare feet.

As people got up from their pews and moved to say goodbye, I braced myself for the comments parishioners might make on their way out of worship. I heard nothing but silence, which to me registered as an even greater possibility that trouble was ahead and that surely I would hear complaints through office visits, phone calls, and lengthy worship meetings in the days and weeks to come. But again, there was only silence.

The silence ended, however, when I happened to be chatting with an older member of the congregation later in the week. We were talking about how much church meant to her, and especially the power of communion. The woman had tears in her eyes as she described how moved she was this past Sunday when our new family had so carefully removed their shoes before going up to the altar rail. Seeing their reverence had brought home for this woman what the ritual meant to her — how, as she put it, she was visibly reminded that God was present, and to consider what it meant to walk on holy ground.

Sometimes we need reminders from others of just how powerful, surprising, and near to us God's presence can be.

Our reading from Acts describes a pivotal moment in the life of the early Christian church, as the message and power of the gospel shifts from within the Jewish community to include all people, Gentile or Jew. But this major shift in thinking, theology and mission happens through a human story, in this case an evocative and thought-provoking interaction between the disciple Peter and the Roman centurion Cornelius.

If there was ever a person who could claim to know Jesus and speak for his ministry, one could argue that it would be Peter. Peter was with Jesus from near the beginning of Jesus' ministry. He heard teachings spoken directly out of the great teacher's mouth; his following of Jesus meant actual steps taken alongside his Savior!

Peter's story in the New Testament is one of great faith and of great shortcomings. Peter famously pushed back against Jesus' prediction of his death, and it was Peter who denied Jesus during Jesus' final days in Jerusalem. And yet, Peter was the "rock" on which Jesus said he would build his church.

As Peter spoke in our reading from Acts today, he was able to sum up the story of Jesus in a concise and powerful way: Jesus preached a message of peace, beginning in Galilee and spreading as Jesus traveled and healed all those whom he encountered. Jesus was killed and was raised on the third day, even appearing to people on Earth after his resurrection.

And now the message is spreading again — proclaimed by the original witnesses to what Jesus did, and being pushed to new places and new people in an ever-widening circle of grace.

I have always been moved by Peter's opening words to Cornelius and his household: "I truly understand that God shows no partiality..." While Peter projected confidence in the message, we who know the full context of the story hear the revelation in Peter's word choice, as if there is a missing "now" that belongs in Peter's words. Remember, Peter had a vision that he was told to eat unclean food; remember that Cornelius sent for Peter. Here is an unlikely pair that God has brought together — not only so that Cornelius could hear the gospel, receive forgiveness of sins, and be baptized, but that Peter's understanding of the mission of the church could be changed as well.

Something had changed in the timeline of the church, this story proclaimed. It is through his interaction with Cornelius — it is through the intersection of their lives — it is through the grace of God that Peter's leadership of the church changed to an even more expansive vision of mission. Cornelius and Peter both needed each other; it is as if they were agents of God's grace to one another — one helping the other understand how God is truly present in that time and place.

Of course, the gospel's mission continues. In this story from Acts, it is not only that Peter's view on the church's mission was expanded, but also that the story of God unfolded in such a way that we are included as well. Indeed, we are witnesses to God's grace that insists on crossing every boundary.

"God shows no partiality," Peter spoke to Cornelius and his household. You do not have to belong to a particular nationality, religious denomination, culture, family or tribe to experience God's presence. We do not have to profess the most complicated theology or meet academic standards either. All such distinctions that humans focus on to separate people do not factor into God's way of sharing grace. Indeed, God has a way of showing up — even when we had given up on such an unexpected surprise appearing in our own lives.

If Peter's faith could be shaped and moved through his encounter with Cornelius, I wonder what effect the people in our world, and on the outskirts of our personal worlds, could have on our faith? Are we open to the continuing movement of God? Can we, like Peter, still learn and be surprised?

I hear the "we" in Peter's mini sermon to Cornelius as both promise and invitation. "We are witnesses." Yes, Peter and the disciples walked and talked with Jesus while he was on Earth, but Cornelius is now joining this "we" also.

When we are baptized, God's grace enters into our presence in a new way — in water and in word, in the beauty of that moment when God is present, and also in the people who surround us and promise to support us in our life of faith.

A community of faith not only helps and encourages us personally, but stand as part of the "we" of which Peter spoke. We point out God's presence to one another; we remind each other that we are all beloved children of God. And somehow, through the grace of God, we experience Christ in our midst.

Through God's grace, we are invited into a vision of the world that shows no partiality. We are loved, and so we love in return.

Amen.

Second Sunday after the Epiphany
1 Corinthians 1:1-9

"I Prayed For You Today"

In my opinion, mornings require a little bit of "zoning out" time. Perhaps some of us just need to lie awake in bed a few extra minutes before we get moving — a quiet transition from sleep to fully awake. Some people like to get up early to do yoga; others enjoy taking the dog for a walk or running on their regular pre-planned loop around the neighborhood before tackling the day. We might watch television, read the newspaper, or simply sip our morning caffeine in silence while the reality of the day sinks in.

Personally, I find that these quiet moments of peace are both necessary and all too infrequent! But when they do happen — when a hush falls over body and mind — it also allows a space to take shape in our lives for something new to emerge.

This idea might sound esoteric or far-fetched, but I appreciate these moments in very concrete ways. When I am quiet in the morning, I might notice how the sun dances around the leaves on the oak trees outside the kitchen window. I can catch the barking of the husky pup that prances down our street, still on the next street over, but excitedly making his way to the end of our block.

In the morning when the day is still fresh and new, I am able to drop the worry of what awaits me in my calendar, or at the destination to which my car is heading. I feel the weight of silence — heavy enough to slowly sink what had been bouncing around my brain and perhaps even to open up a bubble of possibility.

And sometimes, if I am quiet long enough, and even sometimes when I am not, all of a sudden a person's name will pop up into my thoughts.

I wonder how Mitch is doing. The thought can seem like it came from nowhere. Or it can appear just as comfortably as the friend himself, as if he had always been waiting there for me to finally notice.

The names are almost always both familiar and surprising. *Whatever happened to Susan? I haven't heard from Joe this week. Is it too early to call and ask how Tory's treatment is going?* Or, simply, *Cindy.*

This might sound just like the random thought process of the brain, but I have found that more often than not, a sort of emotion develops at the mere mention of the person's name. One thought leads to another, with or without any logic. I begin to think about their situation in life, how they might be faring that particular day, what worries weigh them down, what joys lift them up.

To be honest, I often am not sure why that person's name popped into my head. But I have learned to not let that name go, and instead to continue to think, and remember, and wonder.

Often times, letting the name of a particular person sit in my thoughts shapes itself into a prayer of sorts. These prayers might not sound like the formal prayers we typically label as prayers. But they come from a place and take me to a place that suggests that any label other than prayer is not possible.

I did not always call these experiences prayers, but I have learned to trust they *are* prayers.

I have a priest friend who will often say to me, "I prayed for you this morning." At first, the words would catch me off-guard. What does it mean to have someone pray for you? How do I respond? Do I reply with a "thank you"? Or silence? Should I reciprocate and pray for him, too?

Because I feared I did not know the correct answer for how to respond, I did not say anything. Over time, though, the suggestion that someone else was praying for me influenced my own prayer life. I wondered if I should feel differently, knowing that someone was lifting my name in prayer. I wondered what it would be like to reciprocate, and pray for the giver of my prayer.

I began to take to heart this priest's insistence that each name that took shape and was given voice was held and heard in a very particular way that insisted that the generic become specific, and the open-ended become directional. Praying for peace is wonderful; what would peace look like for Tom? Healing is certainly needed for everyone in this world; how might God's healing touch Anne's life?

Placing the particular in our prayer life can be tricky. We are so afraid of disappointment; so fearful that we will pray the "wrong way." "Am I asking for too much?" I have often wondered, opting instead to simply repeat the big church words I have learned in worship and study, knowing that God will make sense of it all.

Indeed, God does make sense of whatever prayers come of our lives, both spoken and unspoken. And we know God hears our cries, including the names on our hearts and lips that seem to demand our attention and shape themselves into a prayer of their own making.

Rather than question, I will take my priest friend's advice, and let prayers lift up the names on my heart and running through my thoughts.

Saint Paul's letter to the ancient church in Corinth begins with his own name. He is identifying himself as the author and the authority for the advice and wisdom to come, along with Sosthenes, their brother in faith.

When I read these ancient letters, I wonder if the writers had any sense of the enduring audience who would read them across so many generations, continents, and spans of history. Yes, Paul knew he was directing these words to a particular church body, and particular human bodies in that place — some known and some unknown to Paul and Sosthenes. But what of their ongoing lifespan? These words continue to be read, studied, and prayed. For 2,000 years, Christians have taken comfort and been agitated by these ideas put down in solid form so long ago which we still uphold as inspired word and biblical truth — some words upheld much more easily than others.

In this entrance into 1 Corinthians, Paul offers grace and peace from God, and reminds the Corinthians of their calling as saints. Then in some of his most remembered and treasured words from this particular letter, Paul states his thanksgiving to God, and his ongoing and continuing thanks for the readers themselves.

It is difficult to imagine the wideness of this statement by Paul. If we read on in the letter, we know that not all is perfect in Corinth — not even in this church community. And yet Paul gives thanks for them.

I have to imagine that when Paul wrote these words, he was not only giving thanks for their group identity, but also for the gifts of God present in each one of them. He knew some of their particular names, and some of their unique personalities. He knew their struggles and conflicts, and even the points of contention amongst them. And yet, Paul first gave thanks for them.

I cannot imagine all the layers of meaning, and all the steps of logic Paul thought through before composing his letter. But this piece at the beginning shows signs of a true pastor's heart. Paul's words are a prayer, rising up to God, rising out to the people of Corinth, shining light back on Paul as he carefully places himself in the right frame of both mind and heart before writing his letter. He is pausing to create a particular space for God to link author and reader, preacher and listener, teacher and student — all gifted with grace and peace that only God can give.

Indeed, it is this same grace and peace of God that will give enduring power to this letter. It will not only instruct and inspire the Corinthians, but will be passed on and preserved. Even as I read Paul's letter to the Corinthians now, I hear Paul praying thanks for me. And when I preach these words in the midst of the congregation, God's word echoes through Paul to offer thanks for each and every member of the body of Christ who listens — all in whom God takes delight; all in whom we are to continue to give thanks today.

In the early spring of 2021, I listened to church leaders planning worship for a world shaped by a pandemic. We were struggling with our desire to "go back" to what we had done in the past; we were struggling with keeping up the new technologies we had adopted to be able to worship in new ways; we were struggling to connect with church members who were scattered, isolated, fearful, and who felt forgotten. We did not have easy answers as to a smooth path forward.

What we did share was a passionate belief in the truth that God continues to speak — including to us today.

One of the challenges of a passage like our reading from 1 Corinthians is also its gift — this very basic understanding that runs through this introduction of Paul's letter that God's word indeed is very present. Sometimes the words are not clear to us, or we assume we know these familiar words of grace and peace without hearing them in our particular setting. Sometimes the direction of God's word leaves us uncertain as to which way we should go.

Rather than rush to conclusions on what exactly is being said, perhaps we should allow Paul's words today to be a prayer.

So listen to the words again as a prayer said for you... we who call upon the Lord wherever we are; we who seek to see ourselves as individuals separate from others and still linked together in one body — we are all called saints today. To us flow these ancient words as gifts of grace, and gifts of peace.

God hears words of thanks for us, and as we hear these words of a prayer today, we realize how blessed we are to hear such thanksgiving in regards to us. We have been blessed by the richness of God's gifts, and somehow, despite all of our limitations, the good news grows stronger when shared amongst us. We find that we have every gift we need when are called into this fellowship with Jesus Christ our Lord, and that somehow we receive strength to keep us going and renew us each and every day.

This prayer of Paul is now our prayer, too. We are invited to come and see; we are asked to speak and listen; we are asked to hear of God's gifts to us, and, in return, to share such gifts with the world. We give thanks, as God calls us into discipleship for a holy journey that is only just beginning.

Amen.

Where Are Your People?

Many years ago, I arrived at Oshigambo High School in northern Namibia as one of the new high school English teachers. This was the late 1990s, when apartheid was over, but the country still bore very visible scars from years of abusive government rule and all-out war.

I was not the first American to teach English at the school, but I am certain I stuck out like a sore thumb when I first arrived. Despite all the training and advice I had received before I arrived, I did not speak the local language, and I dressed and acted very much like an outsider who was still jet-lagged from a foreign land.

I remember very distinctly meeting the school principal on that very first day. He looked at me, shook my hand, and without missing a beat, very quickly asked me, "Who are your people?"

I think that question made time stand still. Or at least it seemed so to me.

I did not know what or how to respond, but I did know I needed to respond with some answer. My mind raced: Was this a normal getting-to-know-you question? Was his question a friendly gesture, or had I already offended him? Was I supposed to answer with my family name, nationality or culture? Was this an opportunity to talk about the people who had trained me, and the organization that was sponsoring me?

Was the whole question a trick I had missed, or an easy question I just could not decipher?

Or maybe the question was asked because the principal just thought it was so strange to see a person so far away from home and so far removed from the group of people who had brought her into this world and raised her. Perhaps his question pointed to his deeper concerns of why anyone would leave their people to come and be with a new people, and what my motivation to come to this place was really all about.

Who are my people? The question hung unanswered in the air during that first meeting, as I never really did know how to respond, and the principal never came back to his query. I have since wondered the same question many more times as I have moved, changed calls, said goodbye to loved ones, and welcomed new friends and family. "Who are my people?" is a question of who I am as well.

While I failed to answer his initial question, I soon found out the Namibian principal of the high school was also a pastor. I never got a chance to ask him the question in return, but I often wondered why I never thought to answer that I was a Christian, the identity we had in common and which called us both to the same place of service. By many definitions, our people were vastly different, even at odds at times. In the kingdom of God, though, our people all bore the name of Christ through baptism.

Who are your people? In today's passage from Paul's letter to the Corinthian church, we hear repeated comments going around this ancient community that have come to the author's attention. People are saying, "I belong to Paul;" "I belong to Apollos;" "I belong to Cephas." We can only imagine the in-fighting, gossip, and tension that would have led to this reporting of bad behavior making it all the way to Paul's ears.

So much of Paul's letters to the Corinthians seek to settle disputes and sort out problems. So much of Paul's efforts are directed at diffusing tension, seeking higher ground, and holding the gospel up for all to see. In this passage from 1 Corinthians, Paul tried to do all of those things by calling what appeared to be a very splintered group into the unity of their baptism.

Paul did not waste time, did he? Neither did he soften or code his language. No, instead, by repeating directly what had been reported to him, he sought to go directly to the problem. His forthrightness put the labels the community was using in bright and glaring light so that they could be seen, discussed, and corrected.

"Has Christ been divided?" Paul asked. Not only does the language call out the community's division, but the imagery's violence should raise the reader's disgust. "Of course not!" we want to shout. We can even join in Paul's sense of shaming the community, as he thanks God he only baptized a few people within their ranks, and instead raises up his larger mission to proclaim the gospel.

Rather than see this passage as a downplaying of the rite of baptism, however, we can instead appreciate the powerful language Paul utilizes to get his point across to a physically distant audience. The labels the people in Corinth are using for their "brand" of baptism, and their self-identification with particular teachers and leaders in the church are not helpful, but harmful.

They were instead, Paul reminded them, to remember their common identity in Christ, and be held together with the power of the cross.

Much of our own baptismal language in the liturgy still reflects Paul's unifying language here. We intentionally call each other brothers and sisters in Christ; we intentionally call upon ancient words and symbols that have been part of baptism services since our earliest Christian ancestors. We are baptized into one baptism — that we might be united with Christ in this life, in death, and in eternal life as well.

This unity in baptism holds us together as Christian community. And yet, even as we celebrate one baptism and proclaim we are one in the body of Christ, we seem to be more divided than ever. Indeed, Paul's ancient words seem particularly timely now.

The names might be different, but the group identifiers still lure us, and the deep divisions still plague us. Are you from a red state or a blue state? Whose name is on your hat, or t-shirt, or shouts from your yard sign? To which of many flags do you pledge allegiance? Can people assume they know you because of the brand of car you drive, the beverage you drink, or the neighborhood in which you live? Do we want these personal choices serve as labels? Do we want them to set us apart, or to help us find and gather as community?

We might no longer identify as people who belong to Paul, Apollos, or Cephas, but we also might be reluctant or even unable to see our shared identity in Christ.

What divides and unites us can be a very lofty or even philosophical discussion. But it is also a discussion that hits us very practically in our daily lives, including when we interact with the people right around us. For me, I often get time to reflect and process such thoughts on my drive to and from school, work and errands each and every day.

It used to be that I would entertain myself on long car drives by looking at the scenery. Now my entertainment often comes in the form of reading car bumper stickers. Yes, there are bumper stickers for political candidates — some national, some regional, some distinctly localized, some from long ago — thereby dating both the driver and the car! Some of us want to identify with a candidate's optimism or promises; some long for change or shout as an act of defiance.

Some bumper stickers you drive past proclaim allegiance to a particular philosophy or attitude toward the world. Some are very serious, while some bumper stickers are just plain funny.

Some folks have stickers that identify the places to which they have travelled, and the vacation spots to which they cannot wait to return. Some of us have stickers that name our favorite sports teams, hobbies, and heroes.

Some elaborate stickers pay tribute to those loved and lost, like a traveling altar to individuals we miss. Some stickers detail the members of our own families, like a traveling photo album for those who might be inside the moving vehicle.

While I prefer the bumper stickers that make me laugh, I cannot help but also notice the bumper stickers that make me think — even confound me — including the stickers that trouble me, too. There are bumper stickers that make me shake my head, stickers that shout anger, and stickers that divide.

Sometimes the stickers on any particular car are so diverse that they seem to contradict each other, or at the very least suggest a divided household that somehow all rides together in the same vehicle. I always wonder how lively the discussions are in those cars!

No matter my feeling when I read these bumper stickers while driving along, though, I believe the point of each of them is to seek connection to those who might read them and might, in some fashion, feel the same way.

Therein lays both the promise and the problem. Those bumper stickers proclaim an identity that might lead to connection just as surely as they could, in this world of today, identify someone as "other" and different from us.

Clearly the quick labels we place on one another are not enough to promote common understanding, and we need to go deeper to truly engage one another and find what holds us together. There is absolutely a need to "get out of the car" in both a philosophical and practical sense, and get to know the people who are driving all around us.

In a very real sense, now is the time when we need to talk to our neighbor, rather than assume we know the answer to who they are. We must find a way to get past the labels and seek to see one another the way God sees us.

Who are your people? What if Paul was to ask us the same question today? Would we cling to political affiliation, personal heroes, status? Would we point to the "others" around us who are not like us? Would we proudly proclaim what ties us together in God's creation?

As the church, we are people bound together in Jesus Christ. And yet, labels still follow us. While it is good to be proud of our heritage, our denomination, our congregational identity, even the teaching and leadership of our pastor — ultimately, it is in Christ where we find our common mission.

Indeed, unity comes through the gospel — this good news which claims us, changes us, and sends us out into the world. In proclaiming we belong to Christ, we also proclaim that we are connected in beautiful ways we cannot fully understand. Indeed, we proclaim our faith that God has claimed us in such a beautiful fashion that we live our lives in response.

Amen.

Where Foolishness And Wisdom Meet

Right out of college, I took a teaching job at an overseas high school. I was eager to live in a new country and experience adventures in the midst of another culture. Life in Southern Africa was indeed a completely new experience that I could never have imagined before I moved there.

But moving overseas to teach at a high school meant that I did have a job to do, which not only required getting work done, but also it meant having to do many of the daily tasks that make up our daily routines here in the United States. I had to prepare lessons and grade papers for my classes, but I still had to cook meals, wash clothes, and organize my house. This meant I also had to buy groceries, get mail, and get out a broom every once in a while (probably not often enough…).

It sounds silly, but sometimes the more mundane activities of life struck me as the most bizarre when I lived overseas — often because these everyday chores butted up directly against my dreams of a fairytale-like vacation existence. In fact, sometimes the most common tasks of daily life indeed wielded some of the most memorable experiences of that time in my life!

Buying food at an open-air market was certainly never dull, and neither was the line at the post office and the banter from everyone waiting in line. But what struck me as the biggest culture shock was the seemingly simple task of driving a car.

Maybe this is a decidedly American experience, but we Americans do love our cars, don't we? I am old enough to have grown up going for "Sunday drives" with my father, for the sheer pleasure of putting around and exploring if anything in our part of the country had changed recently. My father taught me to identify people by their cars, whether said car was driving down our road, parked by the grocery store, or pulled over in front of our home, and he taught me to love the beauty of each and every car, no matter the model, make, or year.

I grew up loving family vacations that meant driving through multiple states while noting each places's unique license plates, and also loving road trips with friends that took us to the ice cream store just a few minutes up the road. Many of us probably have fond memories of sitting on a parent's lap and pretending to drive, and the first time we were allowed to work the pedals ourselves. Getting my permit, followed by my driver's license, was a teenage rite of passage, marking an important entryway to the freedom of being behind the wheel that I treasure to this day.

In other words, I was used to driving a car and had many years of experience and a deep love for the automobile before I headed to Southern Africa and was given the use of a car to drive when it was necessary.

It sounds easy — what could be more relaxing and simple and truer to my personal identity than driving a car? There was just one small problem: the country where I lived required that I drive on the left side of the road rather than the right.

Unless you have had this experience for yourself, it is hard to explain the sheer gut punch that happens when making one's first attempt to drive a car on the opposite side of the road than what you are used to doing. First of all, the driver's side shifts to the right, the passenger side the left. Imagine getting into the car to drive in this new country for the first time and realizing you have no steering wheel in front of you!

Once I did sit down on the correct side of the car and found myself behind the wheel, the reorientation continued by forcing me to switch the hands that normally changed the radio station and controlled the air system. I won't bother trying to translate my horror at running a manual transmission with the gear shift to my left instead of my right....

But nothing can prepare an American for pulling out into traffic and driving in the left lane instead of the right. Not only did I need my passenger to keep yelling "left, left, left!" at me as a constant and consistent reminder to do what was correct, but I had to fight the voice in my head that was screaming "wrong! wrong! wrong!" For many months, I waged this fierce battle with my instincts in order to drive in this foreign land.

Driving on the left side of the road was not just about learning a new skill, but felt like entering a universe where everything seemed upside down and to run against the very fabric of my being; where the tasks that should have been the most automatic suddenly required great effort.

What do we do when we enter a reality that is contrary to our experience? What do we do when suddenly left is right and up is down? How do we handle something new that tells us our training is not applicable anymore? Where in the world do we find safety when the rules of the road that we have lived by no longer apply?

No one likes to be uncomfortable. Absolutely no one would choose to dwell for too long in a place where life is upside down. And yet, God seems to be calling us into precisely this very uncomfortable place today, where what we have known, and the rules we have always followed, are all called into question.

In writing to the early Christian community in Corinth, Paul points out that these folks would not be the natural power brokers in a community. They were not born into high status, and they were not the wise rulers of that land. Rather than despair in such lowliness, however, Paul lifts up this position as one of ultimate privilege. Indeed, God has called the people of the Corinthian church to hear and proclaim the message of the cross.

The "foolishness" of the cross might be lost on us who are used to seeing crosses on jewelry and as gleaming symbols of beauty and devotion in our church sanctuaries, but the cross would have been seen in a much different light by the Corinthians. For those who lived under the brutal authority of the Roman Empire, the cross was an instrument of violence and humiliation, and Jesus' death on the cross would have echoed the fears of the audience in Corinth who heard Paul's words.

How can a crucifixion stand for wisdom and power for those who are persecuted? How can weakness show forth strength? How can death bring life? How can God choose the Corinthians for this message, rather than those who already seem to be in control in the world?

In other words, Paul's message in preaching Christ sounds like absolute foolishness. And instead of shying away from that truth, Paul doubles down in proclaiming this upside-down message of foolishness as the wisdom of God.

We hear echoes of the Beatitudes in Paul's words — reverberations of Jesus' own sermon on the blessedness of what the world considers foolish and weak. And while the words of blessing in the Beatitudes have become familiar to us, they still speak to a topsy-turvy understanding of the world that hits us like a gut punch when we hear it. We certainly do not feel blessed when we mourn; certainly no one would ever want to be reviled or choose persecution as a way of life.

What is this picture God is painting for us of foolish wisdom and power in weakness? How do we make sense of it, and how are we to respond in our lives once we hear this message of Christ crucified?

One of the images my mind goes to is that of buttoning up a shirt first thing in the morning. If I am half-asleep (and even sometimes when I have no excuse at all), I sometimes mismatch the first button with the corresponding button hole. I never do this intentionally; no, I have tried, by my best estimate, to line up the right and left side of the shirt so as to match perfectly.

But in just being off a tiny bit, I do not notice the mismatch. I button each button on down the line, and it is often not until I get to the bottom of my shirt that I realize I am way off and have messed up the task completely. When I look in the mirror, the shirt looks ridiculous, with one side higher than the other.

Whenever this happens, I shake my head and laugh at not only how I could have made such a mistake, but how I could have gone on for so long thinking that I was correct. Remember — I often button almost the entire shirt before realizing I was

off-set at the very beginning! It takes a picture of absolute ridic-
ulousness to make me see my misperception which began at the
top of the shirt.

Sometimes I seem to live my life the same way. I live most
days thinking that life is perfectly natural and normal. Others
are driving on the same side of the road as me, and I seem to
be cruising along just fine. I have my work, my hobbies, my favorite entertainment, my beloved technology. I pray that God's
kingdom come, but mostly I am content with the way things
already are.

And then suddenly I catch a glimpse of how upside-down
the world is, and I see that the buttons do not all line up in order.
Perhaps it is a moment I am in grief, or when I sense the injustice that others experience in daily life. It might only be a short
moment, and yet I cannot un-see that what I thought was wise is
foolish, and that true power comes from serving others.

When those moments happen — and when the discomfort
settles in; where foolishness and wisdom meet in a cross — in
that precise moment between perishing and being saved — that
very juncture is grace. It is not ours to own or control; I do not
even believe we can make complete sense of it. And yet, in that
moment of grace, God reminds us of a better way — God's kingdom breaking into this world, just as a cross brings forth the gift
of life for the world.

Amen.

Thank God For What We Do Not Know

I believe one of the greatest privileges of being a pastor is to be able to listen to our people's stories. Sometimes the call into ministry gives us access to people who have lived through historic times in places of great opportunity and challenge. Often our call gives us a sacred space to hear how God has moved and the Spirit has shown forth in what have seemed like very ordinary days, in places we only thought of as our normal.

Time and time again, I have been silenced — and moved to awe — by how God shows up in each one of our lives.

On a seemingly normal day, my office telephone's red light was blinking as I stepped inside — a sign that someone had called and left a message for me. I began my regular office routine by pushing the button to listen out loud to the message while simultaneously turning on overhead lights, waking up and logging into my computer, putting down my book bag, and surveying the damage of the paper piles I had left on my desk the day before.

Most of my voice messages are typically routine, and so it makes sense to multi-task and mark things off of my daily to-do list while listening to the messages left on the telephone. Pushing the red button on this particular day revealed, through a sincere and comforting computerized voice, that indeed my office phone had been busy while I was away! I had not one, but five messages waiting for my attention!

Unfortunately, as the computerized voice offered up the recorded calls, it also failed to yield the voice of any living human being. It seemed, upon further investigation, that every call had been a hang-up, and that every call had also originated from the local hospital.

To a pastor's eyes and ears, such a combination of information was quite distressing. Who in the world was trying to call me from the hospital while I was out? Why in the world did they hang up? What was wrong? And why did they try calling five times?

My mind quickly dreamed up all sorts of awful scenarios whereby some very distressed person would not be able to speak from a hospital bed, whether from illness, fear, grief, or even anger that I was not present to answer the call.

It did not take long, however, for the answer to be revealed, as the mystery hospital caller rang once again — this time while I was present and able to answer the telephone myself.

It turned out to be a member of the congregation whom I had just seen at worship two days earlier. She began to tell me the story of the past few days and the many days leading up to this hospitalization. It turned out that she had not told me months ago of her heart condition, had not shared all of the worry that had weighed on her shoulders, had kept in silence the dread that prevented her from sleeping well, and was only now telling me of how all of this stress had sent her heartbeat into an irregular and dangerous rhythm.

The caller admitted that when she had called earlier, she did not leave a message. She went on to say that her lack of leaving a message was not because she was out of breath, and not because she could find no words to share her story. No, she had felt all of those feelings earlier, but really her reluctance to leave a message was because her news was so wonderful she had to tell me for herself in real time!

In that moment, I have to admit that the good news did not start out sounding too good, but worked its way up from the very bottom of this woman's despair. She told me of the extent of her sickness, and of how she kept trying to ignore her symptoms and delay alarm until a call to 911 was her only option. She spoke in a calm, ordered manner of the rapid clip of physical tests, doctor consultations, and difficult conversations that happen in a stressful hospital emergency, and of the ultimate decision to undergo a serious medical intervention to reset her heart's rhythm.

While others might accept a medical procedure as inevitable fact, this patient had become terrified of what could go wrong, and what this medical update could mean for her long-term health.

So in the height of her fear, anxiety, and growing terror at what was to come, the woman grabbed her son's hand, and rather than seek comfort from him, she began to pray to both seek and offer comfort to them both.

Her prayer was one of release — of attempting to let go of all that she was holding on to and taking a deep breath for peace. As she prayed, she recalled to me later, the words of her prayer took on their own life, coming no longer from memory or even rational thought, but pouring out from a place deep inside of her that longed for peace and believed that peace would indeed come from God.

In that moment, she recalled, she was at peace — ready for whatever was to happen once the hospital staff took her away to begin the scheduled procedure.

It was at that moment that a nurse entered the room to study the heart monitor. She was followed by another nurse. And finally a doctor entered, studying the monitor and then proclaiming that the patient's heart had gone back into regular rhythm, thereby cancelling the medical intervention.

My parishioner called to share the good news that the procedure was not needed and that her heart was doing better. I could tell she was relieved that her medical prognosis had changed for the better. But I could also tell that something else had shifted besides her heart rhythm. She had received a peace she had not dreamed was possible, and it had happened in and through the gift of prayer. This gift had worked its way into her very body, and even if she did not understand it, she sensed the wonderful mystery of God's power to change her life in a real and immediate way.

I have to admit that I did not have much to say in response to this parishioner's story, except to praise God for such a blessing.

While parts of my brain rushed to ask questions and understand the event from various angles, there was also a gift that came to me: the need to be quiet and simply listen.

What is God's wisdom? What does the Spirit reveal to us that the world cannot teach? Why do words like those to the church in Corinth both inspire and confound us? How can we sense that they speak truth, even if such truth can be hard to explain in our own words?

Perhaps a line can be drawn from these words of 1 Corinthians to the parables of Jesus. How can we be salt of the earth, and how in the world can salt lose its taste? How are we like light, and why do we hide the light we have been given? Are we like sheep or goats, or are we struggling to figure out what it means to be human? Is the kingdom of heaven far away, or as close as right in front of us? Can we see even a glimpse of what God sees? Can we be certain that God sees, hears, and continues to call us in the here and now?

The mystery of God is so beautiful it humbles us; its words so loud and clear, we struggle to speak them out loud for ourselves.

If I am truthful, I find it difficult to articulate the moments when I have felt the closest to God. I have made a living out of talking an awful lot to other people about God, and yet the moments I would really love to talk about cannot be contained in mere words. But I still know them by their truth.

Sometimes these times of the Spirit's closeness have been moments in holy spaces to which I have traveled far from home, while others have occurred while washing dishes in my very own kitchen. I have felt the Spirit in beautiful cathedrals, remote wilderness, and the Spirit has moved while I have enjoyed the feast of Holy Communion in my own church.

I often think about how God has shown up as I sat at the bedside of the dying, and of Spirit meeting water in the powerful proclamation of baptism. The word shows up in precious bits of holy scripture, and also in the chitchat with congregants who often carry heavier burdens than we ever imagined possible.

So many times, it has taken other people's words for me to find the verbal footing of which I search, as the visions of the faithful meet the gifts of interpretation and proclamation.

These moments when we feel God the closest in our personal experience reveal that the Creator of all sees each one of us — marking us in our uniqueness, and binding us in a common humanity. All of these holy moments together are reminding us to keep listening — to the voices from the margin, to the quiet ones in our midst, to the silence deep inside ourselves, to the buzz underneath the loudest shouts.

I am reminded today to simply say "thank you" — that parishioners have the patience to keep trying to call me And that they want to share their stories. I am thankful that they find peace, not through the work of those who seek perfection, but in this beautiful mystery of God. Thank God for the Spirit which never ceases to show up and surprise us once again.

Amen.

To Grow In God

My son is ten years old, which for him means that he loves to play baseball, is way too eager to play video games non-stop, and would prefer to read comic books rather than a book assigned by his teacher at school.

Being ten years old for my son also means that every morning when he wakes up, he checks his height against the growth chart in his room. You see, he is checking to see how much he grew from the day before. More precisely, he is measuring how much he grew during the night itself.

My son is convinced that such growth is measurable, and, one morning, he will wake up and be screaming in excitement that he instantaneously and mysteriously shot up over six feet tall in a matter of hours.

Each morning he stands, back to the wall, hand on top of head, and pushes back on his hair until the side of his hand touches the wall. He then twists and turns, trying to keep his hand steady in place while he turns his head around to get a good look at where the hand rests on the wall today.

We have caught an occasional yelp of joy in the morning when my son measures his morning height to see that it's higher than the morning before. Of course, this joy is usually much less the following morning, when he realizes he did not measure correctly the day before....

I credit my son's morning height ritual to a few factors. The first is that his sister is two years older than him and did seem to magically grow a foot taller over the course of just a few months. The second is that he has heard many people tell him that he is going to be tall like his father, and that "at his age," he will seem to grow up to be an adult overnight.

So far, he is still waiting for his growth spurt to come. And while I know there is no hurry, he is anxious each morning to measure his height and look for signs of oncoming adulthood. Lately, we have noticed that if the height test does not bring good results, a close inspection of his upper lip almost always seems to reveal to him an oncoming mustache that is only visible to his powerful young eyes.

I know I am physically all grown up, but sometimes I wonder when my spiritual growth spurt will come. Yes, I have been baptized and confirmed. I should be pretty mature, I suppose. Yet I still feel as if these words from 1 Corinthians cut directly to my heart. Am I an infant in Christ? Is it okay to be waiting for spiritual growth, not quite ready for solid food?

As I read Paul's words to the Corinthians in this passage, I get the sense that we are supposed to also hear a subtle message underneath the words. While Paul was writing in a noble and polite way that calls us to a place where we can agree and see our similarities in the gospel, I cannot help but think that Paul would really have liked to have said to the Corinthians, "Grow up!"

We can gather from Paul's statement that he had heard reports of the jealousy and quarreling amongst the group. Different factions within the church were claiming allegiance to various teachers, including Paul and Apollos, and we can surmise that perhaps some regarded themselves as superior in authority or knowledge based on these various allegiances.

Paul reminds the Corinthians that it does not matter who did what in bringing those folks to Christ and teaching them the ways of the gospel. What matters is that the servants of the Lord did what they were called to do so that God might give the growth.

Paul also emphasizes, very smartly, that he and Apollos are both God's servants, "working together." They are not in competition or working for their own glory, but called into common mission to encourage growth in God's people. Therefore, since

Apollos and Paul are able to work together, so, too, the text implies, all the church members in Corinth should be able to work together in growth for the service of Christ.

In speaking about the temptation to jealousies and quarreling, Paul paints these acts in terms of the flesh, as they show an inclination to human behavior. Paul, in turn, wants to call the church in Corinth to spiritual growth. If they are able to grow — including to see Paul's wisdom in this letter, and grow past their current divisions — then they will grow into their lives as spiritual people.

While much can be said about Paul's dichotomy of spirit and flesh, in this passage it serves to remind me that we all have growth we need to aspire to in the spirit. Do we ever find ourselves free from our human tendencies to be jealous of what someone else has? Do we ever refrain from quarrels completely? Rather, it seems that instead of growing in a linear fashion in one direction only, we continue to cycle back and need to be reminded that our growth is not complete.

In other words, I do not know if we ever reach a point where these words of Paul do not speak directly to us.

When confirmation time rolls around in my congregation, I follow the Altar Guild up to the storage space to pick out white robes for our ninth graders who are affirming their baptisms and taking on greater responsibility in the church.

Every time I go up to the closet in which the robes are kept, I am amazed at the wide variety of sizes we have available, all designated by height. We have robes that are marked to fit an individual from 4 feet 2 inches all the way up to over 6 feet tall! And believe it or not, I often have to pick robes from across that spectrum!

Anyone who has ever taught confirmation class knows that the difference in growth is not merely shown in a wide span of heights. There is a tremendous continuum of physical, emotional, and spiritual maturity in middle school youth. While some youth are struggling for independence, others are happily attached to family and school systems. There are youth in the class who are dating, and many who still think dating is gross. Gathered in one classroom are the naïve, the bored, the philosophers and dreamers, the practical realists, the anxious and worried, and even the grieving. Their experiences in life are vastly different, and it can be a struggle sometimes to find a lesson that everyone can engage in and still learn.

As I have taught more confirmation classes and gained more experience as a pastor, I have seen that this continuum of maturity is not only for confirmation students. Every church has members who are reluctant to hear about death and dying, while other members seem to never be able to catch their breath from rolling waves of grief. Some members are confident in expressing how Jesus has changed their lives, while some of us are still waiting to see more with our own eyes.

Not everyone has had the same experiences in life; none of us have lived the life of another. And yet we sit together in the same sanctuary and sing together, pray together, hear the Word of God together, carry one another's burdens. Why? I believe we are each trying to grow.

Part of our growth as spiritual people can be done in very concrete and practical ways. Can we reconcile with our neighbor, rather than insult and fight? Can we learn to control our anger and turn to love rather than hate and hold a grudge? Can we value the dignity of each person and seek equality in our relationships, rather than constantly be driven to compare ourselves to others and appear superior?

There are many times I have wanted to say, "Grow up!" — both to others and to myself. And I wonder if my pursuit for growth for myself and others would do well to remember Paul's words, and to remember that growth comes from God.

As a parent watching my son grow, there is part of me that grieves each milestone. Yes, I am excited to see him reach higher, gain skills, mature, and develop his own sense of self. I also sense my desire to control the how's, when's, what's, and why's of his growth. There is a loss of control I feel as I watch him grow.

I know — I have to let go. I know — growth is inevitable. I know, my faith tells me — it is God watching over this miracle of life as he grows, develops, and needs his parents in different ways. I know that growth was built into him the moment he came into being, and yet I still know how hard it is to let go.

I wonder if a similar sense of control was also part of the Corinthian church to whom Paul wrote. It is one thing to say that God is at work providing spiritual growth in the people. But it is quite another thing for the teachers and leaders to let go of their need to control — not to claim a ministry or group or new members as their own — but to simply give praise to God, and trust that the growth will continue.

Indeed, it remains difficult for us as churches to not try and control growth. We fret over attendance and the dollars in the offering plate, we feel the push for numbers to go higher and higher, and often believe that we are solely responsible for growth. We beam as members show resilience in their faith and step up to greater responsibility. These are all wonderful aspects of growth. But we know we did not do them ourselves; we know we cannot claim the glory. Our faith teaches us that it is God who is at work.

When I consider the exceptional teachers I have had in my faith life — the pastors, instructors and mentors who have guided me to grow — they have all had one thing in common: they were clear that they were serving God instead of padding their own ego.

I hope each one of us has such an experience in the life of faith in a congregational setting. I hope we are each blessed with leaders and mentors who challenge us to grow. And I continue to pray that God grows our hearts, so that we are not driven by jealousies or disagreements, or even by our need to control and be right all the time. I pray that God be given the glory as we stretch and grow as spiritual people.

Amen.

Our North Star

The great leader Harriet Tubman is known to us for her role in the Underground Railroad — the network of safehouses and people who risked their lives to protect and guide escaped slaves in the time before our nation's Civil War. We know of nineteen trips Tubman led which brought seventy enslaved people to their freedom in the north. In her own words, she "never ran her train off the tracks, and never lost a passenger."[1]

Harriet herself had been born into slavery in Maryland, and had lived in a time and place where her very life itself had a dollar value assigned to it by her owner. She endured the suffering of slavery, and was determined to not only free herself, but to also free as many other slaves as possible.

When Harriet was young and was out working, she was struck in the head by a heavy lead weight that was directed at a different slave being punished for attempting to flee. The weight missed the fleeing slave, instead hitting Harriet with a vicious blow. Knocked unconscious and bleeding, Harriet was simply brought home without receiving any medical care.

Harriet's very life hung in the balance for several days following the accident. In time, she did survive the brutal violence of the attack, but for the remainder of her life, Harriet suffered severe headaches and sleeping fits because of this brain injury.

Alongside this physical suffering, Harriet found she was also blessed with visions. Yes, Harriet was a dreamer. She had dreams that she was flying; she dreamed about the life she could live as a freed person. Harriet enjoyed these dreams; she also refused

---

1   Harriet Tubman, Suffrage Convention, New York, 1896.

to let these dreams remain a happy idea, and instead insisted on making them her reality.

As a young adult, she and two of her brothers decided to escape to the north. They traveled at night when no one could see them, but lost their way. Discouraged, they eventually turned back and returned home to life as slaves.

The failed escape did not get Harriet down. No, instead it made her even more determined to escape to freedom.

The story goes that in the time after her first escape attempt, Harriet had another dream — and this time she was not just flying, but flying at night toward the North Star — all the way to her freedom. She left Maryland soon after — by herself — again traveling at night, with only the North Star to guide her. She followed the star all the way to her freedom in Philadelphia.

She had made it! Harriet had fulfilled her dream and flown to freedom!

Harriet's life as a free person did not let her rest, though. She instead set her mind on freeing others. And she would use the North Star again and again on her trips to lead other escaped slaves to freedom in the north.

Harriet is known still today as an emblem of courage and strength. She was resilient, determined, both tenacious and selfless in leading others to freedom. It is no wonder that books, films, and plays have celebrated her life and told her story.

As I read her story again, in our time, I am also struck by her vision to find the North Star in the midst of so much darkness of night and use it to guide her and so many others to freedom. Can you imagine, following the light of a single star? Can you imagine, traveling by its direction, for your very life? Can you imagine, finding that spot in the dark night sky, so that no matter how lost you feared you might be, you always could find your way again?

Stars in the night sky are so numerous we cannot even count them. Here on Earth, we occasionally marvel at their beauty and imagine the vastness and power they represent from afar. But stars remain a source of light that is insignificant to most of us on any given night.

Harriet's story is a reminder that even a single star — even the smallest point of light — is powerful enough to guide the dreamer, the courageous, the dedicated servant to their true destination.

What is the light that we follow? The night can seem so dark to us, stars are hard to identify. But some people can see clearly. And their vision leads us all to true light.

The season of Epiphany is about finding light — begun by the story of wise men that follow a star to the place of a Savior lying in a manger. During this Epiphany, we have witnessed Jesus' baptism, his calling of disciples, his power to heal and cast out demons.

In today's gospel, the light is bright and clear — a vision beheld by the disciples Peter, James, and John on a mountaintop. Jesus was transfigured — changed before their very eyes. They saw him clearly, in line with Moses and Elijah. They heard God's own voice instructing them to listen to his son.

The disciples were amazed. They were also terrified.

The vision before them was so clear that they were given absolute certainty of just who Jesus was, and absolute direction that Jesus was indeed the way of true life.

They were also shown that the way of life Jesus called them into meant they could not stay on the mountaintop. They left that moment of clarity, going down the mountain and following Jesus all the way to Jerusalem. There would be so many times when the disciples would not understand, or would even disagree with what Jesus was trying to teach them.

They would search for their own might; they would question what it meant to serve; they would fail to understand why Jesus had to suffer and die. Their fear would give way to denial, and in dark times, it would be hard for the disciples to remember the bright vision on the mountaintop. It would take the light of an empty tomb at sunrise on Easter morning for them to remember the light that began their journey, and called them to keep sharing light with the whole world.

The author of 2 Peter found it important to echo to his readers the words spoken by God the Father to Jesus: "This is my

Son, my beloved, with whom I am well pleased." The author himself stated that he heard these words at an event we call Jesus' Transfiguration.

Listeners were further instructed to tend to these words of truth as to a "lamp shining in a dark place."

While an oil-burning lamp might be an image that is too old-fashioned for many folks in our modern era, we have probably all had some sort of experience of trying desperately to protect a flame as to keep it from going out. Perhaps we might have diligently attended to a new campfire, or fanned embers to nurse a fire in the woodstove back to life. We might have tried to light many candles on a birthday cake at once with a single match! Or, as church folk, we might have witnessed precarious candlelighting traditions in our own churches.

When I hear the description of this image of paying attention to a lamp shining in a dark place, I cannot help but think of the young acolytes in my congregation who carry a still-flickering flame from the back of the sanctuary, down the center aisle, all the way to the altar in the front of the sanctuary, where they proceed to light the candles that will direct our worship and fill our worship space.

It sounds like a simple task to light candles, and yet it can be terrifying for these youth who are providing service for our worship gathering. The trick is that walking down the center church aisle is also to walk through the "wind tunnel" that happens in church because of the overhead fans — a breeze that you rarely notice until the moment you are in charge of carrying the flame all the way to the candles while it seems like every set of eyes in the congregation is fixed on you.

I have seen many a panicked youngster watch in fervent prayer that the flame does not go out on them. The experienced acolyte has learned to walk faster or slower, depending on where the fans blow. The cautious acolyte has learned to cup her hand around the flame to block any breezes from snuffing it out. The veteran acolyte has learned to trust the process — and remember that the usher is watching from the back and on standby with the lighter…

We know that some days are brighter than others, and that some days hardly shake off their gray dreariness. Some nights are so dark that they seem to carry no starlight at all. Sometimes the lights around us are so dizzying that it is hard to point out the singular light that can lead us on the right path.

But for those who are witnesses to the source of all light — the light that no darkness can overcome — there is always enough light to lead the way.

As we enter into a new season of Lent, we might already feel the way is dim, the days too dark. There has been so much sickness all around us; so much grief that weighs us down; so much that divides us and keeps us apart.

But that does not mean the light is out. And it does not mean that true light cannot be found.

Today — and in the days and weeks ahead — we are called to be people who point to the light and protect it. We might not be as brave as Harriet Tubman. We might not have received the vision of Peter, James, and John. We might struggle to point out and identify the stars in the sky that can lead us forward.

But we each have a story of how a single light on a porch welcomed us home, or the light of the moon that lit our journey on a drive from the hospital. We know the particular way the light from the stained glass windows cast colors onto the church walls. We know the light reflected in our neighbor's face shines in our own as well.

We share this light of Jesus's transfiguration. And when we witness to it — through word and deed — we become changed people, too.

Stories like those of Harriet Tubman and the disciples often seem like distant history to us. But we read them and proclaim them and share them with others because they are our story, too. They have the power to guide us; they have the ability to light our way.

Indeed, as God's people, we can point to the light of prophets like Harriet that still lead us — people who were willing to give of themselves. And we can join in this holy work of tending to lamps, sharing light, pointing to stars in the sky that others struggle to see — all directed to Christ.

Amen.

Freedom Through A Firm Foundation

During a recent visit to my son's elementary school, I was suddenly struck by how much had changed in education since I was a student. Without sounding too much like an old curmudgeon, education is not the same as it was 'back in my day!'

Of course education, like every field, has evolved over time. We know that training, testing, technology, and social factors have all meant constant change for education. But innovation became both supercharged and an absolute necessity when our world went through gathering restrictions related to the Covid pandemic. Almost overnight, school districts had to move to online education to reach, teach, and support students while they were learning at home.

I do not believe there is any way to overstate how dramatic this shift was for teachers, administrators, learners, and their families. Administrators mobilized to acquire and distribute technology to students. Teachers who thrive on seeing their lessons reach students were talking to cameras, often looking at blank screens from students who were invisible on the other side. Families were trying to maintain the order and discipline of school while also doing their own work and chasing family pets seeking attention! Students were trying to learn, connect with friends, and simply feel some sense of normalcy.

Needless to say, the stress level was high all around.

What was amazing to me was the creativity that also abounded during this time. Bus drivers got in their buses and returned to their routes to deliver meals and provide a friendly face to homes. Community leaders brought Wi-Fi hotspots to households who lacked the service. Teachers learned new technologies overnight, bringing enthusiasm to videos and taking extra time to provide support to struggling students — even teaching outside, if that's what it took. And students still found ways to learn and be silly. They also managed to remain kids, who developed unique resilience and also managed to support one another during scary times by having birthday parties by car parade and parking lot graduations.

When I think of how much changed in such a short amount of time, I am truly in awe. To make such strides in technology in a matter of weeks would have been unthinkable before the pandemic, and now has been shown to be accomplished in days.

Yes, necessity forced innovation. But none of the innovation would have worked if not for a shared passion for what was truly important: education, a uniting passion for helping students learn.

We in the church world are not as well known for innovation. We are rooted in ancient tradition and sacred story that has been passed down to us from generation to generation. We have also been known to say, not ironically, that our favorite hymns are from the 1800s and proudly point to fifty-year-old carpet in our fellowship halls that still doesn't look "too bad." In other words, we are not typically the first to jump on the bandwagon of anything new and resembling change.

Of course, the Covid pandemic forced churches to innovate. Like schools, we also made rapid changes in technology, accessibility, and the shape and structure of worship. Even the distribution of Holy Communion probably had to be altered in some fashion in many of our congregations.

I remember thinking during the pandemic time period that it was incredibly stressful to make quick decisions and put them into effect. I also remember thinking that there was a simultaneously odd sense of liberation that our collective resistance to change was forced to soften in light of the public emergency brought on by the pandemic. Churches that had been reluctant to update websites were now livestreaming; congregations that had not wanted a new picture directory were now welcoming online worships and singing over the internet in a cacophony worthy of the day of Pentecost itself.

And in our isolation and loss of all that had been routine, we realized we missed the simple gift of hugs and handshakes and all the hallmarks of community. More than ever, people had a need to hear the gospel proclaimed during such a time of fear.

As gathering restrictions were loosened, new questions emerged. At first, the questions were about what we could do safely. But over time a refrain emerged, demanding to "go back to the way things were *before.*"

I missed pre-pandemic life, too. But I was never exactly sure how to go back to what seemed now to be a dream version of what was never quite our congregation's reality. Was there ever a time when church life was perfect, or easy? And could we simply turn back the clock and erase the trauma of pandemic time?

Like many churches, we have tried to balance innovation with tradition, creativity with comfort, and surprise with safety. We have tried to take a deep breath and determine when change is not just for the sake of change, but for expanding our ability to reach people with the gospel.

All in all, we have been forced to see the need to identify upon which foundation we are building. If the foundation is firm, it will provide for strong growth and innovation and all that the future has in store for us. If the foundation is Jesus Christ, then grace abounds.

Our reading today from 1 Corinthians finds Paul comparing himself to a "skilled master builder." While the title might seem high praise of himself, Paul was careful to proclaim that nothing could be built unless the foundation is Jesus Christ.

By God's grace, Paul was able to lay this foundation of Christ in the Corinthian community. By God's grace, this community grew. By God's incredible grace, we are blessed with these words that continue to have power and provide us with insight and the gifts of the Holy Spirit so many, many years later.

Of course, Paul was writing during his time in response to a problem or concern in the early church in Corinth, which means that not everything was perfect. No, we know that people were claiming some sort of allegiance to various teachers and leaders in the church, including Paul, Cephas, and Apollos. We do not know how the teachings of these leaders might have differed or the extent of how this discord affected the assembly, but we know that the allegiances served to divide the community, rather than unite them in Christ, and thus Paul needed to write on this issue to these faithful people.

Paul called his readers back to what was firm, and on which all faith needed to be built. It is not a matter of teacher or baptizer, denomination or pastor, education or zealousness. No, all of Paul's focus was instead on what gives strength so that building might occur, the cornerstone of which is Jesus Christ himself.

It is an odd concept to digest: that which allows us to grow in faith way up into the boldness of the stars is actually what firmly roots us deep down and keeps us solid. Just as an educator can only innovate and teach others if they have a passion for learning and a love of helping students, so, too, a church can only soar in so much as its foundation is in Jesus Christ.

In a very practical sense, this is why we worship together every week as a congregation, and why we read scripture and pray together when meeting and making decisions. We build our church foundation when we baptize and share in the Lord's Supper. When we focus on the strength of our unifying foundation, we are also open to growing as the body of Christ in new ways.

If I take to heart Paul's words on the foundation that is Jesus Christ, then I need not fear the other builders who come along to add walls and windows, stories upon stories to the strong foundation of Christ. It sounds good, but I consider the many times I have become suspicious of what other leaders are doing, and have thought to myself that "only I" know how to truly build something correctly when it comes to faith.

Put another way, let us imagine that Paul wrote in his letter to the Corinthians that only he knew the way to preach Christ, or that only Paul had the skill involved to properly lay or build on to a foundation. No, instead Paul was clear that the foundation is Jesus Christ, and that all belong to Christ. Within this understanding, therefore, there is no boasting about which human leader did what, since all growth can be traced back to the foundation of Christ.

What an important message for the time in which we now find ourselves! We need not be jealous of another church down the street, or a preacher we see on television. We need not try to copy the music or style of worship we find on social media in a rush to keep up with others.

We do, however, keep coming back to our foundation in Christ. And if we are firm in such a foundation, innovation and creativity will surprise us to grow in new ways we perhaps had never imagined before.

When we focus on Christ, we also let go of our grip on nostalgia. If Christ is inspiring growth in our faith, we will not feel threatened when we try new music or engage in new ministries that reach out to people who need to hear the good news of Jesus Christ. We will welcome people who do not look like us and will encourage new voices that do not sound like our own. We will find room in the choir, space in the pews, seats at the decision-making tables for all who are joined to us in our shared foundational strength. We will be able to not only dream of future growth, but see the Spirit at work in our midst.

I do not have easy answers for where the church is heading in a post-pandemic world. But when I read these ancient words of Paul to the Corinthian church, I think about how these very modern concerns of ours have been echoed throughout time.

As humans, we are apt to jealousies and the need to compare what we have built to what others have built. We are often insecure and just plain afraid of what we might lose if we take a chance and try something new. We have witnessed how division and fear can find a home in our hearts and make us reluctant to reach out and love our neighbor.

But firm foundations allow, support, and encourage growth. And when Christ is the foundation on which our church is built, we truly are free to build.

Remember our foundation in Christ! Grow in his love, and know where our support lies.

Amen.

The Umpire Strikes Again

Baseball season is upon us — again! It is time to cut the grass in that perfect crisscross design, rake the mound, and paint the lines to get the field ready for play. It is time for players to get in shape by perfecting their swing, tweaking their pitching release, and getting to know their teammates' strengths and weaknesses. It is time for fans like me to study lineups, dust off the travel chairs that were in the garage all winter, and work on new cheers for the season.

I do like to follow professional baseball each season, but all of the work I am describing is actually for my son's little league team. Kid baseball is serious now; maybe it always was. I'm not sure why parents and grandparents take such intense interest in this game that our children and grandchildren think of as fun, but we sure know how to pile on the anxiety, don't we?!

Perhaps there is no place of greater scrutiny in what is supposed to be a fun activity than in the role of baseball umpire. These men and women are often volunteers from the community, or paid a nominal fee that hardly seems to come close to measuring up against the stress level placed on their work at home plate.

Every pitch that crosses the plate, of course, needs a declaration from the umpire of whether it is a ball or a strike. While most pitches at this level are pretty obvious and straightforward in their categorization, some require judgment by the umpire.

Was it a ball outside of the strike zone? Was it a strike that curved in over the plate? What will this ump declare on the inside pitch that brushed the batter back off the plate?

Full disclosure: I am terrible at calling balls and strikes. I have not been trained, I have not put in the time and practice, and my reflexes are simply not quick enough to give the snap judgments that are required by the umpire.

My lack of ump skill, however, has never prevented me from professing that I know more than the ump during the game. I like to imagine that, just like it shows on television, there is an outlined box that magically appears for each batter, making it absolutely clear if the ball falls inside for strike, or outside for a ball. I like to also imagine that I can see this strike zone clearly — even if the ump cannot!

Listen — I promise I'm not one of "those" parents…. But occasionally I do feel the need to shout out to the umpire my opinion on whether his or her call seemed correct to me. (And, I am ashamed to admit, I did once offer the ump my glasses so he could see better…). Okay — maybe I am one of "those" parents… but I certainly have plenty of company! Parents, visitors, grandparents, aunts and uncles, brothers and sisters — everyone seems to have their own opinion on how the game should go and what they would do if placed in charge — and they are not afraid to scream it and let their opinion be known to all!

Yes, it seems our youth are not exempt from loud shouts and the strong feelings of some spectators in the stands who want the game to go their own way. It turns out that not all of us are very good examples of sportsmanship for our children. Perhaps we are also not the best callers of balls and strikes, either.

I was recently at a baseball game in which the ump had to stop the game after he heard loud complaints about his own calling of balls and strikes. The complaints from the crowd had been ongoing throughout the game, but at some point the ump had reached his limit. He turned to the bleachers, asked for respect for his job, and reminded the crowd that the players were ten years old. It was only when he threatened to halt the game completely and call it for the visiting team that the home crowd quieted down — including the grandmother who had been yelling the loudest!

Calling balls and strikes is not easy. And for some reason, we seem to think ourselves the best at judging balls and strikes when we sit far enough away to object to the person who has already been placed in charge.

It often takes a complete reset, a truth-telling, a loud reminder of whose job it is to run the game for us to reconsider our protests and realize the need to get our vision corrected. Sometimes that moment comes as a shock, and sometimes it points to a truth we have been carrying for a long time.

In our faith, such a moment means a reorientation to our creator, redeemer, and sustainer, and a release in letting God be God.

When I read Paul's words in 1 Corinthians on being judged, I probably superimposed my own personal experience on to his point of view. I think of the times I have felt judged, or have been quick to judge others. We can create our own continuum of discomfort when it comes to judgment: the sense that others are judging us for a particular action or belief, the grief when we feel excluded, the pain over a declaration by a person of authority that we are wrong and need to correct our behavior or thinking, the shame in being condemned for our actions, or even for who we are.

While much of our discomfort might be in the form of memories from childhood, I have noticed an uptick in recent years in my own perception of others' judgment, and even of my own.

I wonder how I will be judged if I take a public stand on an issue; I worry about others declaring "foul" if I post a belief on social media platforms. I work diligently sometimes to rid my comments from perceived bias that could trigger others, and I weep at the truth that has been lost. Indeed, I wish and pray for Paul's strength of words and faith.

In examining my fear of others' judgment, I am also revealed for the power judgment has over me — specifically, the power I give to judgment when I look at how others' lives differ from my own. I am too quick to assume someone's entire belief system based on a single comment, a single stance on an issue, a single interaction. I am too eager to point the finger and assign blame, rather than being open to my neighbor's life as yet another opportunity to meet God's creation and finding a new way to love my neighbor.

As I consider the many times I have assumed the role of umpire in calling out what I see as balls and strikes, I pray I might take to heart Paul's words. How do I truly believe that only the Lord stands as judge? How do I see my own calling as a disciple of Christ? How do I allow the truth of who God is to change the way I live every day?

Paul did not only speak of judgment in our passage for this week, but also spoke of other key concepts in this passage to the Corinthian church. One is a reminder that we are servants of Christ — a call to which we can never be reminded enough of in this world. We are to serve one another, following the example of our servant Savior.

The other is the notion of a steward. Steward is an old-fashioned word that we will probably not hear in everyday conversation in our daily lives. But to be stewards, as Paul calls us to be, is an extension of our faith.

Stewards are people who take care of something that does not belong to them. If we are, as Paul said in this letter, "stewards of God's mysteries," then we have a role in caring for what God has given to us. No wonder, then, that stewards are required to be trustworthy, since any gift of God is precious.

What is interesting in Paul's words here is that our role as stewards of God's mysteries is not up for debate. In other words, there is not a list of demands we must meet before we are given the ability to care for these mysteries of God. No, if we are already stewards, then God already sees us as worthy of such a calling.

Surely being trustworthy stewards is a heavy responsibility, and yet, we can feel encouraged in the calling as well. In Paul's case, this status as a servant of Christ and steward of God's mysteries somehow reminds him to not feel the slings and arrows of other's judgment, nor be led into judging others based on his own jealousies or insecurities. If he remembers God's calling to him, then he may have confidence in his mission to the gospel.

I wonder what it would mean for us as church if we could let go of our perceived role of moral umpire and embraced the roles of servants and stewards.

How often we fall into the trap of needing to condemn certain people, certain cultural movements, or certain changes in the world that we feel are threatening to our way of life. Such a view suggests not only that we are judge over right and wrong, but also that the world is fixed and that grace does not continue to flow and change the landscape of creation.

Instead of judge, servants look seek not to condemn, but to lift up. Servants approach with humility, knowing that we all fall short of the glory of God. Servants follow a way of care for others paved by Jesus, and live as if God is the only and ultimate judge.

Stewards also see the strength in being called by God. They know the trust God has placed in them, and they work to care for each part of God's beautiful creation, knowing that all is in the hands of the one who breathes life into being.

To be a servant and steward is to let God be God.

Yes, the world is changing, and the pace of change seems to be ever quickening. Yes, it is scary to see culture and country, and even church, changing from what we might remember from years gone by. Yes, it is tempting to wrestle control out of chaos, and shout over the umpire our own perception of balls and strikes that we see from where we sit in life.

It takes tremendous effort — repeating over and over again to ourselves and one another — to place ever before us that God is the ultimate judge, just as Paul reminds us here. It takes tremendous faith and courage — repeating over and over again to ourselves and one another — that we are servants of Christ and stewards of God's mysteries.

But if we are willing to be servants and stewards, we are able to let go of judgment. We can be free to approach what is controversial not with fear, but with curiosity. We can be free to love our neighbor as we love ourselves, with genuine care and concern. We can be open to how God continues to call us trustworthy and commends us for our love.

Amen.

How Grace Finds Us

My childhood home has a large picture window set into the living room. The home still stands in the middle of a Minnesota prairie, on land my family homesteaded generations before me. The window looks out onto our front road, the gravel road that marks the edge of the property, and beyond that on to the flat fields that stretch on endlessly beyond the horizon.

When I was growing up, most days the curtains would be wide open so that anyone who sat in the living room could look out and catch any excitement going on, which in this rural part of the country, often wasn't much. More exciting, I found, was to look out at the fields and imagine what might happen. Would a friend come to visit that day? Would someone new drive past our house? Would an animal wander by, or a storm approach?

It sounds quite boring, but looking out of that window was a popular pastime for me and my siblings growing up.

The large picture window had another role for me in my childhood, in that it was the place I would run to when I was in trouble. More specifically, I would run and hide in the curtains that hung over that large picture window.

Isn't it strange the odd details we can remember from childhood? I can remember clearly the bright green and blue of those curtains, the smooth white backing only visible from the outside, the heaviness that kept them lying straight and seemed to weigh them to the floor.

Whenever I got in trouble, and often before I had been caught for doing something I knew was trouble, I would run to the picture window and hide in the curtains. I even had a very precise way of starting at the edge of the curtain and turning around until I was completely wrapped up in the roll of this fabric.

It seemed like a wonderful hiding spot.

Of course, my logic would be found to be flawed. It was pretty easy to notice the outline of a person wrapped up in the curtains, especially in the feet that were sticking out the bottom. It was also very likely to provoke more anger when caught, since there was the danger the hiding person would strain or even pull down the curtain from the rod above.

But the most obvious and silliest reason that these curtains were not the best hiding spot was that they were covering a clear window. All one had to do was walk by the outside of the house, or happen to be driving by on the road, and see that a person was right there in the window, for all the world to see.

"There is no distinction, since all have sinned and fall short of the glory of God." I have heard these words, read these words, preached these words, used these words in conversation and in comforting people in despair many times, and yet they still have the power to cut through me and remind me of God's truth.

In writing this letter to the Romans, one of Paul's concerns is that the gospel is not limited to one group of people, but that, indeed, it is for both Jews and Greeks. Paul has come to this moment by seeing the good news of Jesus Christ change the lives of people, just as his own life had been so radically changed.

Paul's emphasis on the power of the gospel is worthy of highlighting. These words, these ideas, these stories of Jesus — indeed Jesus' life, death, and resurrection themselves — were not like anything else in all of creation. No, the words Paul preached — the good news he offered to all who would listen — hold power.

As Paul continued, this power is God's power of salvation, available to all who have faith. It is not our works — it is not our obedience to the law that brings salvation. No, it is God who does the heavy lifting for us, so grace might come as gift, and that all might be saved.

Good stuff — actually, this is possibly Paul's finest work. We get it and we love hearing this. But we still have a hard time accepting it.

During seminary, I worked for a non-profit which matched volunteers with other non-profit organizations. My group was an offshoot of a particular denomination, and had the denomination's name in our organization's name. After cold-calling various non-profits, I realized that being tied to a religious group could be confusing to other groups who were not faith-based.

They would often ask if their group had to be religious in order to receive a volunteer, or if the volunteers would be "overly religious," I guess meaning that they would proselytize at work. I would carefully explain that while we were faith-based, our goal was not to impose our belief system on others. I learned to emphasize terms like "shared values" and "focus on service" rather than on the faith that did hold the group together.

Changing my cold-call strategy seemed to help get my foot in the door so I could discuss how volunteers could benefit the mission of various groups. Once non-profits could see the respect we had for their work, they tended to be more open to having a faith-based volunteer.

I would not say I was ashamed of the gospel, but I would agree that I did not promote the gospel openly when I went about my work. That all changed, however, when I met with the leader of a non-profit one day to discuss the next steps in matching a volunteer to her group.

When this leader saw the materials I placed in front of her, she immediately fixated on the name of our denomination in the title. I tripped over my own tongue for a while, until I could launch into my apology and explain what service meant to these volunteers.

The leader of this non-profit listened patiently, and then she asked me specifically about Martin Luther, and how his beliefs were shaped by his study of passages like this one from Romans.

As I sat and listened to this woman speak, I think my mouth dropped open. She went on to explain that while she was not

Christian, she greatly admired these teachings, and told me her own experience of grace.

It was a powerful encounter, as I saw the power of the gospel work through another person.

Perhaps that is the power of the gospel. It does not exist in a vacuum, nor does it float around removed from people. Yes, it is the power of God, but it is power that seems intent on encountering human beings — speaking to them, calling them to proclaim, and changing lives through grace, through faith, through salvation.

We often underestimate the power of the gospel — until it grabs hold of our hearts once again.

Sometimes I remember the young girl who would run and hide in the curtains of the picture window. She was afraid of being caught, afraid of being punished, afraid of being found. She assumed she would be met with anger; she realized she deserved some form of correction, since she knew she had done what she was not supposed to do.

I hate to tell you this — but she was always found. Sometimes a parent would find her and the truth would come out; sometimes a sibling would find her and turn her in; sometimes she would grow tired of hiding and would come out on her own.

When I look back now, I do not recall the punishments, but I do recall the forgiveness. It is not that I never got in trouble, but maybe I do not remember those moments as vividly because they matched the story of what I thought would happen. No one is ever able to anticipate, it seems, the true power of grace.

My clearest memory of being wrapped up in those heavy curtains was when a friend came to visit. I do not recall what I did that was "bad," but I do remember doing something to hurt him and then running to the curtains to hide.

As I waited for my punishment, I imagined not only how upset my parents would be, but also how upset my friend's parents would be. Without the ability to complete the equation yet, I only had the ideas of math that imagined punishment growing exponentially by the minute, as I continued to hide in those curtains.

But instead of my mother finding me, my friend found me first. And instead of screaming "I found her" and running to tell my mother, or lifting up the curtain to shout "gotcha!" he instead went to the opposite side of the curtain, and wrapped himself in rolls until he reached the spot nearest me.

"Is this your hiding spot?" I remember him asking me. "Yes," I said. "No one can find me here." Of course, this was obviously no longer true, since he was standing right next to me.

He continued to stand next to me in silence for a good long time, until we agreed that we were bored and should go back to playing outside again, which we did.

My friend showed me grace that day, even if we did not know that word yet. Rather than rush to punish, rather than show how much better he was than me, rather than point and laugh, he simply met me where I was. He asked why I did the things I did, and he listened to me. He still wanted to be my friend and he proved to me how to be a good friend.

That is grace, my friends. And it is more powerful and vast and all-encompassing than we can ever imagine.

Perhaps it is not the best image, but I think at some point in our lives, we have each been that lump in the curtain, trying to hide from the punishment we believe we deserve. We are afraid and hope no one will notice us, even when our feet are sticking out from the bottom of the curtains, and the window is clear for all to see.

God meets us in that place — exactly where we are — with good news so powerful that often it is nearly impossible to believe. It is good news that is eternal, and it is powerfully good news we all need to hear, right here and now.

Amen.

www.ingramcontent.com/pod-product-compliance
Lightning Source LLC
LaVergne TN
LVHW091200080426
835509LV00006B/766